CASE STUDIES IN
CULTURAL ANTHROPOLOGY

GENERAL EDITORS

George and Louise Spindler

STANFORD UNIVERSITY

THE HURON

Farmers of the North

Second Edition

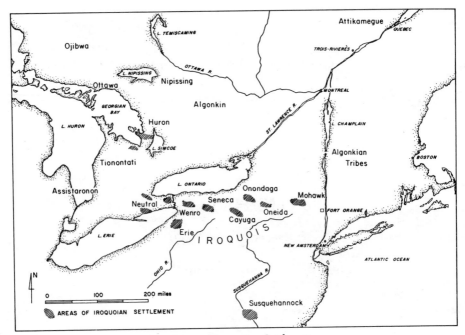

Areas of Iroquoian Settlement

THE HURON

Farmers of the North

Second Edition

BRUCE G. TRIGGER

McGill University

HARCOURT BRACE JOVANOVICH COLLEGE PUBLISHERS

Fort Worth   Philadelphia   San Diego   New York   Orlando   Austin   San Antonio
Toronto   Montreal   London   Sydney   Tokyo

Publisher :	Ted Buchholz
Acquisitions Editor :	Christopher P. Klein
Senior Project Editor :	Dawn Youngblood
Production Manager :	Ken Dunaway
Art & Design Supervisor :	Vicki Mc Alindon Horton
Cover Designer :	Vicki Mc Alindon Horton

To Barbara

Library of Congress Cataloging-in-Publication Data

Trigger, Bruce G.
  The Huron.
  (Case studies in cultural anthropology)
  Includes bibliographical references.
  1. Huron Indians. I. Title. II. Series.
E99.H9T7   1990   306'.089'975   89-24412

ISBN: 0-03-031689-8

Address Editorial *Correspondence To:*	301 Commerce Street, Suite 3700, Fort Worth, TX 76102
Address Orders To:	6277 Sea Harbor Drive, Orlando, FL 32887-6777 1-800-782-4479, or 1-800-433-0001 (in Florida)

Printed in the United States of America

Harcourt Brace College Publishers
The Dryden Press
Saunders College Publishing

7 8 9 0 1 2 3 4 5 6 090 17 16 15 14 13 12 11 10 9 8

Foreword

ABOUT THE SERIES

These case studies in cultural anthropology are designed to bring to students, in beginning and intermediate courses in the social sciences, insights into the richness and complexity of human life as it is lived in different ways and in different places. They are written by men and women who are professionally trained as observers and interpreters of human behavior. The authors are also teachers, and in writing their books they have kept the students who will read them foremost in their minds. It is our belief that when an understanding of ways of life very different from one's own is gained, abstractions and generalizations about social structure, cultural values, subsistence techniques, and the other universal categories of human social behavior become meaningful.

ABOUT THE AUTHOR

Bruce G. Trigger is Professor of Anthropology at McGill University in Montreal, Canada. He was born in Preston, Ontario, in 1937 and obtained his B.A. degree from the University of Toronto and his Ph.D. from Yale University. Professor Trigger has carried out archaeological research in Egypt and the Sudan, and his interest in the ethnohistory of eastern Canada dates from his undergraduate days at Toronto. His books include *History and Settlement in Lower Nubia* (1965), *The Children of Aataentsic: A History of the Huron People to 1660* (1976), *Natives and Newcomers: Canada's "Heroic Age" Reconsidered* (1985), and *A History of Archaeological Thought* (1989). He was elected a Fellow of the Royal Society of Canada in 1976 and in 1985 was awarded the society's Innis-Gérin Medal for his "distinguished and sustained contribution to the literature of the social sciences." Most recently he has received a prestigious Killam Research Fellowship from the Canada Council, which will enable him to carry out a comparative study of the social institutions of early civilizations.

ABOUT THIS CASE STUDY

Twenty years ago we wrote in the foreword to the 1969 edition of this case study, "It is with special delight that one encounters a lively and relatively complete account of a (Native American) culture whose bearers became virtually extinct more than three hundred years ago. In this case study the Huron, an Iroquoian people of great significance in the cultural development of aboriginal North America and in the early phase of European and Indian contact, come to life once again."

Our delight has not diminished and is reinforced by the new insights brought into the case study by Bruce Trigger. More is known about the Huron now, through the study of hitherto ignored information recorded by early observers, archaeological work, and new ethnological insights that have become part of the resources available to the ethnohistorian.

The author's aim is to reconstruct a detailed picture of Huron life in the first half of the seventeenth century. The Huron, victims of various romantic fables, have been cast as avaricious traders, as cowards, and as disorganized, in order to account for their defeat and near extermination by their enemies— the culturally nearly identical Iroquois. Bruce Trigger ignores these myths and "describes the Huron way of life as it appeared when it was first observed by the French." The target date for the reconstruction is 1615, when the first detailed description of Huron country and culture was provided by Samuel de Champlain, who visited Huron country between August 1615 and May 1616.

Particularly notable in the author's reconstruction of the Huron way of life is their preoccupation with personal independence and economic equality. Huron culture contained an "elaborate set of positive and negative social sanctions which served to inhibit the development of economic and political inequality". This characterization raises serious questions about some of the assumptions of an evolutionary model that transforms small interpersonal and group differences into classes and ranks with power wielded by a few individuals.

There are many aspects of Huron culture and society that impress us as anthropologists. Particularly impressive to us as psychological anthropologists are the culturally patterned techniques in Huron culture for maintaining individual balance. The culture provided channels through which the idiosyncratic needs of individuals could be met, sometimes in a spectacular manner and often in ways that transgressed normal sanctions on behavior. As students of Native American culture, we view the inventions by others for the maintenance of psychic security and personal satisfaction with special interest.

In this and other ways we may see in Huron culture, as remote in time and origin from our own as it is, a reflection of our common-human and contemporary problems. The Huron solved these problems in their own unique manner, but in ways recognizable to us.

GEORGE AND LOUISE SPINDLER
Series Editors
Stanford University

Preface to the Second Edition

The present edition of *The Huron* is much altered in content, analysis, and style from the original one. The last twenty years have seen a remarkable increase in knowledge of the seventeenth-century Huron resulting from the development of ethnohistory, the vast expansion of Ontario Iroquoian archaeology, and, most recently, the ethnosemantic study of old dictionaries, grammars, and Christian texts recording the Huron language. As a result of this research, much that was uncertain in 1969 has been clarified, and the understanding of the Huron has become increasingly independent of what is known about the Five Nations Iroquois and other northern Iroquoian groups.

In the first edition, I attempted to familiarize readers with the problems of historical ethnography by drawing attention to the biases of French sources and the speculative nature of many interpretations of data. Because ethnohistorical methodology is now widely known and many interpretative problems have been resolved, the present account of Huron culture is much more categorical.. While it is not possible to justify every statement that is made in a brief ethnography of this kind, an explanation of the positions I have adopted can be found in my books *The Children of Aataentsic* and *Natives and Newcomers*. Elisabeth Tooker's *An Ethnography of the Huron Indians* permits those who are interested to trace the sources for particular statements about Huron culture that are found in the writings of Champlain, Sagard, and the Jesuit missionaries. It does not cover archaeological and ethnosemantic sources.

The first edition was written in the immediate aftermath of Richard S. MacNeish's substantiation of the *in situ* theory, which maintained that the northern Iroquoian cultures had evolved in late prehistoric times from hunter-gatherer societies that were indigenous to the Lower Great Lakes region. It was also written when neo-evolutionism was at the peak of its influence in anthropology. A reflection of both trends can be seen in my tendency to interpret any suggestion of non-egalitarian behavior in Huron society as evidence of an incipient development toward a ranked, or even a stratified, level of social organization. Twenty more years of data collection and analysis have convinced me that this approach misrepresented the nature of Huron society. An alternative interpretation is presented in this edition, which accords better with the factual evidence and with what is known about the cultural ecology of slash-and-burn horticulture in other areas that have low population densities.

Other changes reflect the possibly transient declining influence of psychological anthropology and the more recent adoption of structural and post-structural approaches by anthropologists. I have reduced my reliance on once popular psychological interpretations of Iroquoian data and adopted a more critical stand towards them. At the same time, I have intensified my efforts to relate patterning in Huron beliefs to that found in their social organization. This has helped me to realize more completely my original goal of presenting Huron culture as "a working system."

As a result of preparing this edition, I appreciate more fully the vast amount of work that has been accomplished on the Huron during the past twenty years and also to what extent anthropology itself has changed. I hope that my extensive revisions of this book adequately reflect the positive accomplishments of this period. Limitations of space and the desire to provide a factual account of Huron culture have precluded comments about various research projects relating to Huron culture that are currently in progress. These bear witness to the continuing dynamism and future potential of this field.

I wish to thank John L. Steckley for reviewing the Huron words used in this book, as well as for the enriched understanding of Huron culture that I have gained from his published and unpublished studies of Huron ethnosemantics. Huron technical terms and most names are cited in the standardized orthography and forms he has proposed. Where more familiar spellings have been retained, Steckley's forms are appended in brackets. My understanding of Iroquoian culture has also benefited from discussions over the years with Alexander von Gernet, who was formerly a graduate student, and is now a SSHRCC post-doctoral fellow, at McGill University, as well as with Barbara Bender, Leland Donald, Richard B. Lee, and Steadman Upham.

Susan Weeks prepared the frontispiece and Figs. 2 (below), 9, and 16. Fig. 2 (above) and a photograph of the map *Novae Franciae Accurata Delineatio*, from which Figs. 1, 6, 8, 14, 15, 18, 19, and 22 are reproduced, were supplied courtesy of the Public Archives of Canada. The significance of the drawings that accompany this map for an understanding of Huron culture was first recognized by Conrad E. Heidenreich. Fig. 12 is reproduced from *Les Voyages de sieur de Champlain*, 1613; Figs. 4, 7, 13, 17, 20, 21, and 23 from his *Voyages et descouvertures faites en la Nouvelle France*, 1619; and Figs. 5 and 24 from Lafitau's *Moeurs des sauvages amériquains*, 1724. These are all taken from originals in the Redpath (now the McLennan) Library, McGill University. Fig. 10 is reproduced from James B. Griffin, *Archeology of Eastern United States*, with the permission of Kenneth E. Kidd and the University of Chicago Press, and Figs. 3 and 11 are from my book *The Children of Aataentsic*, with the permission of McGill-Queen's University Press. The first edition of this book was completed while I was recipient of sabbatical leave from McGill University and a Canada Council Leave Fellowship. The second edition was completed while I held a Killam Research Fellowship. I also thank Marta Steele for preparing the index.

I dedicated the first edition of this book to my wife, Barbara M. Welch, as a wedding present. It is my pleasure to renew this dedication after twenty wonderful years, with the hope that what is past may be a happy prologue to what lies ahead for both of us.

BRUCE G. TRIGGER
Montreal, Quebec
June 1989

Contents

1/Introduction

In 1610, the French began to visit the four confederated Iroquoian-speaking peoples they called the Huron. They found their settlements strewn across a small peninsula located between Georgian Bay and Lake Simcoe, in southern Ontario. The prosperity of the Huron was unmatched by that of any other native group the French had encountered along the Saint Lawrence River or in Ontario. Their populous settlements, often surrounded with palisades, were larger and more stable than were the encampments of the Algonkian-speaking nomadic peoples who inhabited the rocky, lake-covered regions to the north, an area rich in fish and game, but little suited for agriculture. The rolling hills of the Huron country supported a prosperous horticultural economy, and the Huron were accustomed to trade their surplus produce with the Algonkian hunters of the north.

For a brief period in the first half of the seventeenth century, the Huron played a key role in the history of eastern North America (Trigger 1976, 1985). Because of their connections with the peoples who lived in the vicinity of the Upper Great Lakes, they were able to supply the French with vast quantities of beaver pelts. In return, the Huron secured European kettles, knives, and hatchets, which they recognized as being more efficient than their own, as well as beads and other trinkets. All of these goods were much desired by themselves and by neighboring peoples.

Between 1610 and 1650 many French explorers, traders, and missionaries, all of them adolescent or adult males, made the hazardous journey inland to conclude treaties with the Huron, encourage them to trade, and save their souls. Unlike most modern anthropologists, these visitors did not find themselves living among groups who had long been influenced by Europeans and who were under the surveillance and control of a colonial administration that had altered their way of life to accord with European standards of propriety. On the contrary, they became the guests of native people over whom they had no political control and among whom even the Jesuit missionaries exerted little influence before 1645. In this exotic environment, individual Frenchmen found themselves alternately scandalized, repelled, and fascinated by the behavior of indigenous people who remained uninfluenced by beliefs and standards they had never questioned. Many came to know the Huron well and developed at least a working understanding of the principles upon which their way of life was based. The vivid accounts that some of these men recorded provide the most detailed information available prior to 1650 about the culture of any native North American group. No other native group in eastern North America was described in such minute detail so soon after contact with Europeans. Comparable data concerning the Five Nations Iroquois, who lived south of Lake Ontario and were culturally very similar to the Huron, are not available until after 1650. The curious juncture of colonial policy, trade, and missionary zeal that led to the documentation of the Huron has thus contributed significantly to our awareness of the native cultures of the eastern woodlands of North America at the very beginning of recorded history. Before we examine the Huron of this period, however, it is important to understand what is being described from a historical perspective.

HISTORY

It used to be thought that the Huron culture had remained unchanged for many centuries prior to the seventeenth century. Archaeological research has demonstrated that this was not so. The Huron way of life had already changed in response to the presence of Europeans in North America before it was first described by the French and had been changing rapidly for many centuries prior to the arrival of the Europeans. What the early French visitors described was not a static culture but merely one phase in the development of a way of life.

The theory that the Huron and related northern Iroquoian-speaking peoples had arrived in the Lower Great Lakes region as a single group only a few centuries prior to the historical period and had brought with them a culture that had originated in the southeastern United States is no longer supported by archaeological and linguistic evidence. Rather than being intrusive, the northern Iroquoian cultures were created by hunter-gatherer peoples who had long inhabited the Lower Great Lakes region. Linguistic evidence indicates that the northern Iroquoians were already split into ethnic divisions roughly corresponding to certain of their historically known peoples long before a horticulturally based way of life had been adopted. The Seneca, Cayuga, and Oneida languages were already separate by A.D. 800 at the latest, while the split between these three Iroquois languages and Huron must have occurred considerably earlier (Lounsbury 1978). The evolution of the historical Iroquoian cultures can thus be viewed as a process of parallel development involving a number of peoples speaking related languages.

Prior to A.D. 1000, the peoples who lived in the vicinity of the Lower Great Lakes subsisted mainly by hunting and fishing. Several hundred people might assemble at productive fishing camps between spring and autumn, but these bands dispersed in small groups to family hunting territories during the winter. Around A.D. 500, corn was introduced into the region. After that time horticulture slowly became more important, and small palisaded villages that were lived in year-round began to appear. At first these villages were thinly but relatively evenly dispersed throughout the areas bordering the Lower Great Lakes. The fact that adjacent Iroquoian-speaking groups were able to communicate with each other more easily than with Algonkian speakers may account for the many cultural innovations that came to be shared by the different Iroquoian peoples. Although nearby Algonkians participated in the development of various features of "Iroquoian culture," they did so to a lesser degree. The Algonkians who lived to the north of the Huron were also excluded from participating in many of the basic features of the Iroquoian way of life by environmental factors.

After A.D. 1300, Iroquoian settlements grew larger, and their inhabitants became increasingly dependent on horticulture. Beans, which are rich in proteins, were now planted along with corn, which provided carbohydrates but was lacking in calcium, niacin, and tryptophane. Excessive reliance on corn alone resulted in deficiency diseases, such as pellagra and childhood cortical bone loss (Pfeiffer and King 1983). After they had adopted a more varied horticultural diet, the Iroquoian population increased rapidly and soon began to approximate the levels known in historical times (Warrick 1989). Multifamily houses also became larger and palisades more heavily fortified. Still later, cooked human bones began to appear in middens, suggesting more intensive warfare, even if at this time most raids may have been directed against nearby communities. Warfare promoted defensive alliances and encouraged the clustering together of villages to form larger peoples or nations and, still later, the joining together of peoples to form confederacies. As a result of these developments, the cultural uniformity of southern Ontario began to break down. By A.D. 1400 a culture ancestral to that of the historical Neutral and Erie peoples can be distinguished north and east of Lake Erie, while another one ancestral to that of the Huron and Tionontati is found distributed in a triangle between Georgian Bay, the Toronto area, and the head of the Saint Lawrence River.

French writers recorded little about the historical lore of the Huron. In 1640 the Huron told the Jesuit missionary Jérôme Lalemant that the Attignawantan and Attigneenongnahac peoples had founded the Huron confederacy over two hundred years (many generations) before, and that the Arendahronon had joined it about 1590 and the Tahontaenrat as late as 1610. If this report is correct, the nucleus of the Huron confederacy may predate the formation of the Iroquois league.

Within the area of prehistoric Huron and Tionontati settlement, numerous clusters of prehistoric sites can be observed. Most of these consisted of only a few settlements none of which can be demonstrated to be ancestral to a specific Huron people known in the seventeenth century. The material culture of the village clusters found in Simcoe County, near Georgian Bay, and farther east in the Trent Valley was somewhat different from that found north of Lake Ontario. The Huron later claimed that the Attignawantan and Attigneenongnahac were the largest of the Huron peoples because over the years they had incorporated more small groups than either the Arendahronon or

Tahontaenrat. This suggests that the four Huron peoples known in the seventeenth century were not immutable entities but groupings that had evolved over time as various communities had come together (Ramsden 1977).

It has been suggested that the Attignawantan and Attigneenongnahac may have been the original inhabitants of northern Simcoe County (Wright 1966:78-80). The claim that these two peoples were able to point out to Jesuit missionaries the sites of their former villages going back for two hundred years seems to support this idea. Through amalgamation, many of the Huron groups that had lived in the Toronto area prior to 1550 may have been absorbed into these two groups. The Arendahronon appear to have been made up largely of groups that in the late sixteenth century had lived in the Trent Valley, and the Tahontaenrat may have come from the south. While each of the Iroquois tribes continued to inhabit its own territory in upper New York State after it joined the Iroquois confederacy, all of the groups who lived north of Late Ontario and in the Trent Valley had abandoned their ancestral territories and relocated in northern Simcoe County by the beginning of the seventeenth century. The Huron continued to use the land that these groups had formerly occupied as hunting and fishing territories.

The movement of so many additional people into the area between Lake Simcoe and Georgian Bay in the course of the sixteenth century must have affected the distribution of the indigenous inhabitants of that area. The continuing need for adjustments may explain why in historical times there was no clear-cut relationship between the areas occupied by the various Huron peoples and natural geographical features. The highest density of prehistoric settlements in northern Simcoe County was in the hilly country near Lake Simcoe (Heidenreich 1967:23). It may have been from there that many of the Attignawantan and Attigneenongnahac shifted into the western part of the Huron country as later arrivals moved in from the south and east.

Two historical questions remain unanswered: (1) Why did all the Huron ultimately choose to settle near the shores of Georgian Bay, and (2) why did the Huron peoples locate their settlements side by side, while the Iroquois peoples chose to keep theirs apart from one another?

The traditional explanation has been that the Huron were forced to flee to where they were living by the seventeenth century to escape Iroquois attacks. There, with their backs to Georgian Bay, they were imagined to be making a last stand against their enemy at the time when they began trading with the French. The Huron were obviously concerned about Iroquois raids and carefully fortified their villages most exposed to attack; although all the Iroquoian peoples did this. Support for this hypothesis has been found in the claim made by the French explorer Samuel de Champlain that the Arendahronon had abandoned the Trent Valley because of their fear of the Iroquois. Moreover, in 1639 the Wenro, an Iroquoian-speaking people from New York State who were being attacked by the Iroquois, fled to the Huron country where they settled in several Attignawantan villages.

It may be that fear of the Iroquois induced some groups to move north in order to escape their attacks. This does not explain, however, why a substantial number of Huron lived in northern Simcoe County beginning as early as A.D. 1300. The theory also seems to be based on an incorrect assessment of the military capabilities of the Huron in relation to the Iroquois. Prior to when the Iroquois began to acquire more guns than the Huron were able to, in the early 1640s, the latter were never at the Iroquois' mercy. Year after year Huron raiding parties entered the Iroquois country and returned with prisoners to be tortured to death. Moreover, the Iroquois peoples were at war not only with the Huron but also with the Susquehannock to the south and with various Algonkian peoples to the east and northeast. In spite of this, the Iroquois were not driven to settle near one another, and rare was the time when all five Iroquois peoples united to fight against a common enemy. While the outbreak of war with the Iroquois may explain why groups such as the Arendahronon and Tahontaenrat wished to be on good terms with the other Huron peoples, it does not provide a reason for them to have settled in northern Simcoe County. Instead, some quite different reasons deserve serious consideration.

From an Iroquoian point of view, the Huron country had many natural advantages. Although the region was colder than the land just north of Lakes Erie and Ontario, there was a vast amount of light soil there. This was the kind of soil that the Iroquoians preferred because it was easy for them to work. Similar soil was available elsewhere, but its particular abundance in the Huron country may explain why some groups had lived there for a long time. The Huron country had other unique advantages. It was surrounded on three sides by lakes and rivers that abounded in places where fish could be caught easily throughout the year. Fish constituted the main source of protein in the Huron diet.

Even more important, the Huron country was located on the very edge of the Canadian Shield and at the south end of the only along-shore canoe trail leading to the north. In the latter region lived the Algonkian hunters, who had a surplus of hides, furs, and dried fish and meat to trade with the Huron, as well as exotic items, such as pieces of native copper that they procured in trade at Sault Sainte Marie and farther west on Lake Superior. These groups were anxious to obtain stores of corn to sustain them over the winter, as well as tobacco and other products from the south. There is archaeological evidence of contacts between the Huron country and the north beginning in early times (Ridley 1954), and it appears that a symbiotic relationship had developed between the inhabitants of these two regions. This interdependence, as well as the friendly relations that consequently prevailed between them and the northern Algonkians, goes a long way toward explaining why the Huron chose to settle in the southeast corner of Georgian Bay (Trigger 1962). The objection that a nomadic people would have been more likely to move toward an agricultural one than the reverse (Heidenreich 1967:16) ignores the uniquely favorable location of the Huron country on the edge of the Canadian Shield and at the head of an important water route to the north.

While the main cluster of sites containing European trade goods occurs within the restricted area where the earliest French visitors reported the Huron were living, a smaller number of more dispersed sites are found to the south and east of this region. Some of these sites may have been hunting camps and resting places used in the historic period, but most appear to date from the late sixteenth century, when only small quantities of European goods were reaching the Huron. These sites indicate that Huron settlements were less concentrated in late prehistoric times than they were in the seventeenth century. It is possible that the final clustering, when settlements were restricted to the Penetanguishene Peninsula and along creeks flowing north into Georgian Bay, resulted from the intensification of trade with the north that came about as European goods were carried inland in ever greater numbers by way of the Ottawa Valley and Lake Nipissing, and the Algonkians began to exchange them with the Iroquoian peoples of southern Ontario in return for beaver pelts.

Unfortunately, the same European visitors whose goods helped to shape the development of the Huron confederacy also set in motion a chain of events that was to disperse the Huron and many neighboring peoples. Unfamiliar diseases, including measles and smallpox, were carried from European settlements into the interior. As a result, beginning in the early 1630s, tens of thousands of Indians died, and many native groups vanished as distinct entities. Moreover, as beaver became exhausted in upper New York State, the Iroquois, who traded with the Dutch along the Hudson River, sought to expand their hunting territories. This transformed mutual raiding between them and the Huron into bloody warfare. In the course of this warfare, the Iroquois, who were able to secure more guns, soon gained the upper hand.

In the spring of 1649, after suffering a series of defeats of unprecedented severity, the Huron decided that their situation had become untenable and abandoned their villages. Many perished at the hands of Iroquois scalping parties as well as from famine and other privations; others found refuge among neighboring tribes. A large number ended up living with the Iroquois, who welcomed them as a means of increasing their own numbers. Most of these Huron settled in existing communities, but the least numerous Huron people, the Tahontaenrat, along with some of the Arendahronon, were allowed to establish their own town, called Gandougarse, in Seneca territory. In time, the Huron who joined the Iroquois identified themselves with their conquerors. Joseph Brant, one of the greatest Mohawk leaders of the late eighteenth century, was reported to have been descended from Huron through both his father and his mother.

About six hundred Huron Christians, the survivors of a far larger number of people who spent the winter of 1649–1650 living on Gahendoe (*Yahwendoye*, now Christian) Island off the coast of the Huron country, settled under French protection on the Ile d'Orléans near Quebec City. Six years later they were transferred to the mainland, where they continue to live today. Although these people ceased speaking Huron about a century ago, they have retained a lively sense of their identity and in recent years have been showing a renewed interest in their history and culture (Vincent 1984).

Many Huron, particularly Attignawantan, sought refuge among the Tionontati, a people who lived a short distance to the west of them along the south shore of Georgian Bay and whose language and culture were similar to their own. Soon, however, the Tionontati, together with these Huron refugees, were driven out of southern Ontario, again with heavy loss of life, by the Iroquois, who did not wish to see Huron trade fall into the hands of yet another native group. For fifty years the survivors of this exodus, who numbered about eight hundred and were mainly Tionontati, lived in the vicinity of Lake Superior. During this period they had close contacts with the Ottawa, Potawatomi, and other Algonkian-speaking peoples, and their way of life was much influenced by these hunter-gatherers. In 1701 the French persuaded many Huron and Tionontati to settle close to Fort Pontchartrain, which they were building where Detroit is now located. Eventually some of these Indians began trading with the English, to whom they became known as the Wyandot, a corruption of Wendat, the former name of the Huron. Some of the descendants of the Huron-Tionontati continue to live around Detroit, but most of them now live on the Wyandotte Reservation in Oklahoma. They, too, have abandoned their native language. It was still spoken, however, by a few people at the beginning of the twentieth century (Barbeau 1960).

With the rapid development of an interest in the history of North America in the nineteenth century, the Huron suffered the inevitable misfortune of the vanquished: They became victims of romantic fables. Historians, who were impressed by the success that the Jesuit missionaries claimed to have had among them, contrasted the apparent docility and peaceableness of the Huron with the bloodthirsty ferocity of the Iroquois. Other historians attributed the downfall of the Huron to their cowardice and contrasted their "disorganization" and "love of trade" with the aggressiveness and hardy discipline of their foes (Parkman 1867). Such myths obscured rather than explained the Huron and their culture and did a disservice to the understanding of the Iroquois as well. The aim of this book is to ignore these myths and to describe the Huron way of life as it appeared when it was first observed by the French.

SOURCES

The following chapters will describe Huron life soon after their earliest direct contact with the French, which began in 1608. Unless stated otherwise, our account will refer to 1615, the year when the first detailed description of the Huron country was provided by a European visitor. By that time all the Huron had settled in northern Simcoe County, but they had not yet become as dependent on European technology, and hence on the fur trade, as they were to be after the 1620s. Nor had they been influenced by missionaries. While most of the data on which this description is based were collected between 1615 and 1650, changes that occurred during this period will be ignored. These changes are described in detail elsewhere (Trigger 1976, 1985).

Descriptions of seventeenth-century Huron culture were not written by the Huron, who were illiterate, but by Europeans who visited the Huron country prior to the latter's dispersal and recorded what they saw there. Historical ethnographers are at an obvious disadvantage because they are unable to observe firsthand the people they are studying. Nevertheless, when written sources are abundant, they can treat them in much the same way as ethnologists do their informants. Different statements can be cross-checked against one another and compared with what is known about the closely related Iroquois and Wyandot cultures at a later period (Tooker 1964). In this way it becomes possible to reconstruct a detailed picture of Huron life in the first half of the seventeenth century.

The principal descriptions of Huron culture are found in three sources. The earliest is Samuel de Champlain's account of his visit to the Huron country between August 1615 and May 1616. During this time he spent approximately five months living in a number of Huron settlements and accompanied a Huron military expedition against the Iroquois. Champlain was a soldier, explorer, and cartographer who devoted the last decades of his life to supervising the development of the French colony along the Saint Lawrence River. Prior to coming to Canada, he had traveled in the West Indies and acquired firsthand knowledge of the Spanish colonies in the New World. The trading companies for which he worked were aware that the fur trade was of paramount importance for the economic development of New France, and because of this he was instructed to win the friendship and respect of the Algonkian-speaking peoples who lived in the fur-rich regions north of the Saint Lawrence and of their Huron allies. In order to do this, he was willing to hunt with these Native Americans and to fight with them against their enemies.

Champlain was not only a skillful geographer but also a careful observer of the native peoples he encountered. While his account of the Huron is not particularly long, it provides a valuable picture of their way of life. Since he was particularly interested in persuading Huron chiefs to trade with the French, it is not surprising that the most successful portions of his account are those describing the Huron economy. As an unquestioning supporter of the French monarchy, he dismissed as chaotic and ineffectual any type of government or legal system that differed from that with which he was familiar. His strong religious convictions also led him to pour scorn on Huron religion.

Our second informant was a man of completely different temperament. Gabriel Sagard, a Recollet friar, arrived in the Huron country in August 1623 and stayed there until May 1624. Since he was unable to convert the Huron, he spent most of this time mastering their language and observing their customs. He published these observations in a book entitled *Le Grand Voyage du Pays des Hurons*, one of the first book-length ethnographies. Sagard recorded his observations concerning the plants, animals, and people of the Huron country. Unlike Champlain, he did not hunt or fight alongside the Huron, although he did accompany a fishing party to Georgian Bay, nor did he manage to visit many of the Attignawantan settlements. Nevertheless, his account is unique. If many years of work among the Huron were to make the Jesuits more familiar with the details of Huron beliefs, none was to record as careful a picture of everyday life as it was lived in a Huron settlement as did Sagard.

Our third source is *The Jesuit Relations and Allied Documents*. The *Relations*, which were published annually in Paris to encourage support for Jesuit missionary work in New France, provide a chronicle of Jesuit activities among the Huron between 1634 and 1650. From 1635 to 1638, these reports were written by Fathers Jean de Brébeuf and François-Joseph Le Mercier. During the early years of their mission, the Jesuits were trying to understand the broad outlines of Huron culture, and their writings are filled with general descriptions of Huron life. Brébeuf and Le Mercier both had temperaments that were well suited to the difficult work of these years. Their writings reflect warm personal involvement with a people on whom their teachings as yet had little influence. Both men were also gifted writers, and their descriptions of Huron life often are of superb quality.

In 1639 the writing of the Huron *Relations* was taken over by Father Jérôme Lalemant, a new superior of the mission who had just arrived from France. He did not have as many personal dealings with the Huron and judged their way of life to be dirty and unpalatable. In writing his annual reports, he devoted most of his attention to describing the growth of the Christian church in the Huron country. The clash between Christian and native beliefs caused him to be interested in only one aspect of their traditional culture, Huron religion. His successor, Father Paul Ragueneau, continued to describe the development of the church and provided a vivid running account of the Iroquois attacks that finally destroyed the Huron confederacy. Ragueneau had a keen intelligence and excellent critical faculties and, like Lalemant, recorded much valuable information about Huron religion.

The Jesuit *Relations* are especially valuable because they represent a study in depth of Huron culture. Being well-trained scholars, the Jesuits were careful to record not only their general conclusions about the Huron but also many of the observations on which these conclusions were based. In spite of this, anthropologists must not imagine these Jesuits too much in their own image. They were in the Huron country to win converts, and their attempts to understand the Huron way of life were pragmatic ones directed toward this goal. It is significant that, although they lived among the Huron for many years, they never understood the difference between peoples, clans, and lineages, nor did they take account of the fact that the Huron kinship system was significantly different from their own. These concepts do not appear to have been sufficiently important in their dealings with the Huron to compel the Jesuits to attach much significance to them. Likewise, the Jesuits record practically nothing about Huron subsistence activities and very little about trade and warfare, except as these activities provided them with opportunities for contacting other tribes. However, the Jesuit *Relations* provide much information about Huron law, government, and religion.

Further information about Huron life is found in various letters written by priests and laymen who worked in the Huron country (Gendron 1868;

Thwaites 1896–1901, *passim*); as well as in Pierre Boucher's (1664) history of New France; Father Pierre Chaumonot's (1869) autobiography; and Father François Bressani's Italian synopsis of the Jesuit writings concerning the Huron.

All of the major descriptions of the Huron were popular works designed to acquaint European readers with what was going on in the New World and to elicit their financial and moral support. They were works of propaganda first, and works of history and anthropology only second. The Jesuits collected far more information about the Huron than they chose to record in their annual accounts; there is evidence that ethnographic material contained in drafts of their *Relations* was excised from the published versions, either for reasons of taste or more likely because there was fear that it would bore readers. There is little hope that most of this material can be recovered. In spite of such shortcomings, the accounts of Champlain, Sagard, and the Jesuits make available a wealth of information about the Huron that would otherwise have been lost.

Knowledge of the seventeenth-century Huron is not limited, however, to narrative descriptions. A vast amount of information about their way of life is contained in Huron grammars and dictionaries compiled by French missionaries. The oldest surviving work of this sort is a phrase book that represents the accomplishments of Sagard and at least one other early visitor to the Huron. The most important works were produced by Jesuit missionaries, beginning with linguistic pioneers such as Jean de Brébeuf, Antoine Daniel, and Pierre Chaumonot. New missionaries would learn Huron by copying out existing studies and incorporating newly acquired knowledge into their work (Hanzeli 1969). Among the oldest surviving Jesuit manuscript sources is a French-Huron-Onondaga dictionary dating from ca. 1655, while the most recent are a Huron grammar, dictionary, and collection of religious compositions copied and revised by Pierre Potier, who worked among the Huron and Tionontati near Detroit from 1744 to 1781. In recent years the linguist John Steckley has been studying the Huron language and has begun to extract ethnosemantic information from the illustrative phrases contained in these works. This research has already helped to clarify the nature of seventeenth-century Huron clan organization (1982a), house structure (1987a), and religious beliefs (1978, 1989), as well as the meaning of place names. Continuing research on this immense corpus of material promises to reveal much more about Huron culture and also, by studying Huron culture through their own language, about the limitations of the understanding that the French had of it.

Another important source of new information is the continuing archaeological research on historical Huron sites (Latta 1985). Major surveys of site locations have been carried out and a number of settlements wholly or partially excavated. This provides important information about settlement patterns and household organization. Other studies have investigated Huron subsistence patterns, ecological adaptation, population trends, and changing patterns in the use of European trade goods. The physical anthropological study of human skeletal remains that archaeologists are recovering adds to our knowledge of Huron health and longevity in the early seventeenth century (Molto 1983; Patterson 1984). Rapidly increasing archaeological documentation of sociopolitical changes in prehistoric times is also helping to set these discoveries into historical perspective (Dodd 1984; Warrick 1984).

Twenty years ago it was widely believed that anthropologists already knew as much about the seventeenth-century Huron as they were ever likely to know. Today, as a result of rapidly accumulating ethnosemantic and archaeological data, it is obvious that, in many respects, our understanding of the Huron culture of this period is only beginning.

2/The Land and the People

The Huron called themselves Wendat, meaning "Islanders" or "Dwellers on a Peninsula." This name has been interpreted as referring to the large bodies of water that surround the Huron country on three sides. It may also incorporate an allusion to the Huron belief that the whole world was an island supported on the back of a turtle. The name Huron is derived from the Old French *hure*, which meant literally a boar but figuratively a rustic or hillbilly. This term seemed appropriate for the Huron, who, when the French first met them early in the seventeenth century, were not as acculturated to European ways, and in particular, did not wear as much European clothing as did the Montagnais and other peoples who dwelt nearer to the east coast of North America.

The Huron, like most of the native peoples in southern Ontario and upper New York State, spoke one of the related languages that linguists classify as Iroquoian, a term derived from, but not to be confused with, Iroquois. The latter is an Algonkian name commonly used by the French and English to refer to the Five Nations of New York State, all of whom were Iroquoian-speaking. The Iroquoian languages of the Lower Great Lakes region are distantly related to Cherokee, which was spoken in the southern Appalachians, and to Tuscarora, spoken nearer the coast in North Carolina and Virginia (Lounsbury 1978).

All the Iroquoian peoples of the Lower Great Lakes region inhabited a single ecological zone of deciduous forest with coniferous admixture, the evergreens becoming more abundant toward the north. These people had much in common: the same basic material culture, a similar economy and social and political institutions, as well as religious beliefs and practices that were closely parallel. Although many individual traits that are associated with the Iroquoian cultures were shared with adjacent non-Iroquoian peoples, the high degree of similarity among the northern Iroquoian cultures distinguished them as a group from their culturally far more varied Algonkian-speaking neighbors.

THE PEOPLE

The Huron were described as well-proportioned and, on average, taller than Europeans. Cripples and other deformed individuals were rare, but were not entirely absent; dwarfs, for mythological reasons, often served as shamans. While, prior to the coming of the Europeans, the Huron did not suffer from many epidemic diseases common in Europe, such as smallpox, measles, and chickenpox, and the French judged them to be a healthy and robust people, physical anthropological evidence indicates that tuberculosis was common in at least some communities, along with a variety of other chronic infections that would have been particularly debilitating during periodic food shortages (Pfeiffer 1986). In addition, probably largely as a consequence of the considerable starch content in their diet and low standards of dental hygiene, dental caries were rampant, and there was much tooth loss (Patterson 1984). Skeletal evidence also indicates numerous injuries. Life expectancy at birth was between twenty-five and thirty years, and few individuals lived more than fifty years (Jackes 1986). Childhood mortality was high because of dietary inadequacies, poor personal hygiene, and the unfavorable sanitary conditions resulting from overcrowded houses, failure to clean eating utensils, dirt floors, and sharing living quarters with animals. Many women died as a result of complications associated with childbirth. Hence, despite the absence of many illnesses familiar to Europeans, the Huron were not particularly long-lived or healthy.

Huron men had little facial hair and carefully plucked out what there was. They regarded such hair as ugly and a sign of inferior intelligence. They also disapproved of curly hair, another instance where their taste proved disadvantageous to the French. The French praised the acuity of the Hurons' hearing and vision, their sense of direction, and their powers of reasoning and memory, the latter being most conspicuously displayed in their ability to remember long and complicated speeches. On the other hand, they were said to be indifferent to the smell of anything they did not eat, such as flowers and perfume.

The Huron were proud of their hair and spent much time looking after it. Women wore theirs in a single tress that hung down the back. The tress was tied with a leather thong or eel skin. Men wore their hair in a variety of styles. Some arranged it in two large rolls above the ears, with the intervening area cut short; others shaved both sides of their head, leaving a roach down the center. Still others cut their hair in ridges, or permitted one side to grow long while they cut the other. Men and women rubbed their hair with sunflower oil, and some colored it with various paints.

Men and women greased their bodies with oil and animal fat to protect them against sun, cold, and insects. On special occasions colors were added to make body paint. The preferred colors were black and red, which were made from soot and bloodroot or red ochre, respectively. The designs that were painted on a person included pictures of human beings and animals as well as stripes and geometrical patterns. Some of these covered the whole

Figure 1. Huron clothing. A family converted to Christianity is shown praying. From the map Novae Franciae Accurata Delineatio, *attributed to the Jesuit missionary F.J. Bressani, 1657.*

body and were so well executed that at first glance the French mistook them for suits of clothing. Some Huron, especially women, were tattooed, but the latter practice was not as common among the Huron as it was among the Neutral and Tionontati.

Huron clothes were made from well-prepared deerskins and beaver pelts. In hot weather a man wore only a breechclout made of deerskin and a pair of soft moccasins. Complete nudity, such as was common among the Neutral and some of the Algonkian peoples, was not acceptable among the Huron. In addition, a man frequently wore a tobacco pouch that hung behind his back. This pouch served as a repository for any charms he might wish to carry with him. In winter, men also wore leggings that reached as high as the waist and sleeves that were held in place by a cord tied behind their backs. On top of this was a skin cloak. Huron women dressed the same as men did, except that in addition to a breechclout they wore a skirt extending from the waist part way to their knees (Fig. 1). In the summer they left their bodies bare from the waist up.

The Huron were trained from their youth to endure hardship and misfortune with patience and fortitude, and to avoid public displays of excessive joy, anger, and fear. Their self-control may account for the often-repeated French comment that they were cheerful and contented but "at all times a little taciturn". They were also restrained and considerate in their dealings with one another. Anger and hostility were directed mainly against foreign enemies and prisoners of war. The Europeans alleged that the Huron, and especially Huron men, were lazy. This appears to have been a false impression created by the division of labor among the Huron, which was not in accordance with the labor routine to which the French were accustomed.

THE HURON COUNTRY

The Huron settlements were concentrated in an area that measured no more than fifty-six kilometers east to west and thirty-two kilometers north to south (Fig. 2). The entire country could thus be traversed in a leisurely fashion in three or four days. On the east the Huron settlements were bounded by Lake Simcoe, on the west by Nottawasaga Bay, the southernmost extension of Georgian Bay. The Huron country was separated from the region to the north by Matchedash Bay, a narrow inlet also opening onto Georgian Bay. These three bodies of water, together with the rivers and swamps along its southern border, provided natural boundaries for the zone of Huron settlement.

A number of small lakes were scattered through the Huron country, but the largest (Cranberry Lake, Orr Lake, and Bass Lake) were located near its southern limits. Five short streams flowed north through this region into Matchedash Bay. From west to east these are now called the Wye, Hog, Sturgeon, Coldwater, and North. Farther east the waters of Lake Simcoe flowed through Lake Couchiching and into the Severn River to enter Matchedash Bay from the north.

The Huron country was located on the northern limits of what is now the rich farmland of southern Ontario. The area of Huron settlement is underlaid by Trenton and Black River limestones and covered with deep glacial tills. The soils that have developed on the tills and outwash are mainly sandy and well drained, but because the material from which they were formed contained more Precambrian rock than was usual farther south, these soils differ from the normal gray-brown podsols of southern Ontario and more resemble the brown podsolic soils to the north. Most of the soils in the more elevated regions are classified as Vasey sandy loams and are moderately stony, while the soils in the valleys, where the land is not swampy, are Tioga sandy loams, which are generally stone free. Both types of soil tend to dry out quickly and are poor in potassium, nitrogen, and phosphorus. From the Huron point of view, however, they had the great advantage of being easy to work. Intractable clay soils are found in the Nottawasaga drainage that marked the southwestern border of the Huron country (Hoffman *et al.* 1962; Chapman and Putnam 1966:299–300).

Immediately north of the Huron country, beginning at the eastern end of Matchedash Bay, the landscape changes. The deep deposits of till vanish, and the hidden Paleozoic limestones of southern Ontario give way to the exposed metamorphic rock of the Canadian Shield. This rock is covered only

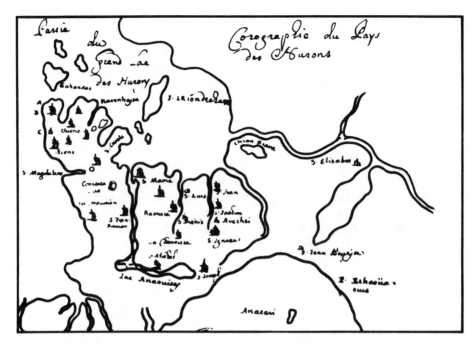

Figure 2. Above: the Corographie du Pays des Hurons, *the best large-scale seventeenth-century map of the Huron country, shows the region between 1639 and 1648. For problems involved in interpreting this map, see Latta (1985). Heidenreich (1966:113) suggests that it may have been drawn by Jérôme Lalemant. The names on the map are those assigned to the Huron settlements by the Jesuits.*

Below: a modern map showing the location of some of the major Huron settlements at the same period.

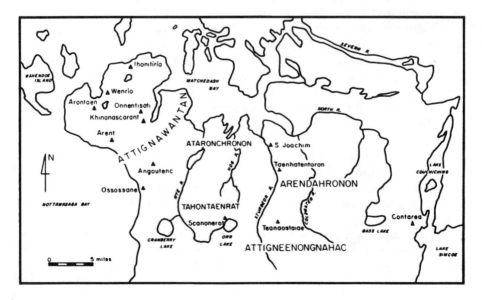

by scattered and often infertile patches of soil. Today this is a land of summer cottages and vacation resorts; three hundred years ago it was the hunting and fishing territories of the northern Algonkians.

The western section of the Huron country is undulating, but nowhere does the land rise more than 155 meters above the waters of Lake Huron. In the north, especially around the heights overlooking Thunder Bay, the land rises quickly from the lake, but near the shores of Nottawasaga Bay are vast low areas, once covered with sand dunes and stunted vegetation. To the east there is a ridge of high ground between each of the rivers flowing north into Matchedash Bay. The northern ends of these ridges were scoured by glacial Lake Algonquin, exposing large tracts of boulders, which made these areas unsuitable for settlement. Nearer Lake Simcoe the terrain becomes hilly and in places rises to over 400 meters above sea level.

The original forests of the Huron country consisted mostly of maple, beech, and oak, with white pine growing mainly on abandoned clearings. Various other kinds of evergreens grew in the interior and in moister areas. Cedar, which the Huron used to construct their houses, grew in swampy areas abundant throughout the region. Other trees found in the Huron country include elm, birch, basswood, and ash. The clearing of these forests in the nineteenth century resulted in a considerable decline in the water table and the drying up of many small creeks and springs. In the "dry hills" of Oro township, in the eastern part of the Huron country, the drop in the water table was as much as nine meters. A similar drop in the water table following Huron forest clearance may help to explain why prehistoric, but not historical, sites are found in that region.

Today southern Ontario has a temperate climate with four well-marked seasons. The climate of the Huron country is not as favorable, however, as it is farther south near Toronto or along the north shore of Lake Erie. The temperature of the Huron country is lower than in these areas, but less so in summer than in winter. The daily mean temperature in the Huron country in July is 19° C., in January, −7° C. The mean annual frost-free period is 138 days, and the growing season 195 days. This is long enough to assure a successful corn crop most years, but the margin of safety is less than in the Toronto area, where the growing season lasts 205 days. About 35 centimeters of rain fall between May and October, and in general, the rainfall is less in March and April than it is during the growing season. This has the advantage of permitting the soil to dry out quickly so that it can be cultivated early in the spring. The snowfall in the Huron country is abundant: 254 centimeters per year as compared with 178 centimeters around Toronto. The average depth of snow in winter is 65 centimeters. The available evidence suggests that the climate of the Huron country was much the same in the seventeenth century as it is today, although it might have been slightly colder.

POPULATION

It is notoriously difficult to estimate aboriginal populations from historical data. Detailed statistical information is normally lacking, and the figures that have been recorded, even seemingly precise ones, are often based on fleeting impressions. It is difficult enough for individuals to judge the population of towns or the size of crowds in their own culture; in an unfamiliar one the problems are multiplied.

The total population that is quoted for the Huron prior to the epidemics that began to decimate them in 1634 is 30,000. This figure has been accepted as reliable because it recurs in the writings of Champlain, Sagard, and the Jesuits. Its origin, however, deserves to be carefully scrutinized.

Champlain informs us that the Huron had "two thousand warriors, not counting the common mass, which amounts to perhaps thirty thousand souls." This indicates a population of approximately 32,000. He did not claim that this was his own estimate; rather he stated that it was a figure quoted to him by the Huron. It is strange that in a society in which all men, or at least all young men, were warriors the latter should have constituted less than seven percent of the total population. The main argument in favor of this figure is that Champlain, after traveling through the Huron country, was willing to quote it.

Sagard stated that there were 30,000 to 40,000 Huron. This suggests that he either copied Champlain's figure, but believed it to be too low or, more likely, included the Tionontati in his total. Brébeuf continued to use the figure of 30,000 prior to his return to the Huron country in 1634, suggesting that it was the estimate of Huron population that was generally accepted by the French at that time. Since, prior to 1640, the work of the Jesuits was mostly confined to the western part of the Huron country, it is questionable whether they were in a better position than Sagard to judge the accuracy of this figure.

The most important statistical data concerning the size of the Huron population come from the Jesuit *Relation* of 1640. There Jérôme Lalemant records that in 1639 the Jesuits visited all the Huron and Tionontati settlements to gather information that would be used for the reorganization of their mission system. As part of this survey, the priests are said to have made a house-by-house census of the entire region. The Huron and Tionontati were together found to have thirty-two settlements, containing 700 cabins, 2000 hearths, and 12,000 inhabitants. Since two nuclear families shared a single hearth, these figures suggest that there were about 4000 families.

These summary figures must be used with caution. There are historical reasons for suspecting that this survey was not as thorough as Father Lalemant's brief description implies. Yet the low overall population and the unnaturally low figure of three persons in each family are not unreasonable, since the census was taken after a succession of severe epidemics had swept the region. Similar epidemics killed large numbers of Indians in other parts of the New World (Dobyns 1983); hence, it is likely that over half the Huron had perished prior to the end of 1639. Figures given earlier in Jesuit *Relations* suggest that in normal times a Huron family consisted of between five and eight people. Assuming that the figure of 2000 hearths provides an accurate indication of the number of families in the region at the beginning of 1639, and that there was an earlier 20 percent loss unaccounted for by these data, we get a combined population of 28,800 for the Huron and Tionontati prior to the epidemics of the 1630s. The relative proportion of the population that should be assigned to each of these two groups is unknown. The Jesuits write of 10,000 Huron after 1640, which suggests that the Tionontati numbered about 2000 at that time. Yet, even if all but one or two of the Tionontati settlements were hamlets, their nine villages, as compared with the Hurons' twenty or more, suggest that this Tionontati figure is too low. Assuming that 9000 Huron survived the epidemics, one can estimate a pre-epidemic population of about 20,000 Huron. While the available archaeological evidence does not indicate significant population decline prior to the 1630s (Warrick 1989), it is possible that at the time of Champlain's visit the population was somewhat higher. Much more research remains to be done on the historical Huron population, and future archaeological data have an important role to play.

SETTLEMENT PATTERNS

A basic unit of political organization was the -ronnon, which signifies people, nation, or what anthropologists used to call tribe. Like the Iroquois, whose confederacy was made up of five nations, the Huron consisted of at least four peoples, each having its own territory, councils, customs, and history. The main difference between the Huron and Iroquois confederacies lay in the distributions of their settlements. Among the Iroquois, the settlements belonging to each people were separated from the rest by stretches of forest that were used as hunting and fishing territories; among the Huron, the different peoples lived side by side and appear to have shared a common hunting territory which stretched south to the shore of Lake Ontario and from the Toronto area east to the head of the Saint Lawrence River. The much greater proximity of the Huron peoples seems to have resulted in more intermarriage and a greater pooling of culture than was the case with the Iroquois. Linguistic variation was also less marked among the Huron. French visitors agreed that they spoke a single language. Nevertheless, Sagard noted variations in the language spoken in different parts of the Huron country, and there is specific evidence that the Tahontaenrat dialect was different from that of the Attignawantan (Thwaites 1896–1901, Vol. X:11). These differences must have developed at a time when the communities that made up the Huron confederacy were geographically, as well as politically, separated from one another. Significant differences were also noted among these peoples in their religious practices; the Attigneenongnahac being renowned for the number and complexity of their rituals. With these, however, borrowing seems to have been leveling out cultural differences.

Champlain was unaware that the Huron were composed of different peoples. He referred to them collectively as Attignawantan, which was the name of the westernmost Huron people. Sagard distinguished three peoples: the Attignawantan, the Attigneenongnahac, who lived southeast of the Attignawantan, and the Arendahronon (sometimes called the Contarearonon [*Ekontareiaronnon*]), whose settlements were located still farther east, near Lake Simcoe. The Jesuits noted still another people, the Tahontaenrat, who occupied a single large settlement near the center of the country. According to the Jesuits, these four peoples made up the Huron confederacy.

The Attignawantan (*Atinniawenten*), or Bear People, was the largest and most powerful of these groups. About half of the Huron belonged to this nation, which appears to have also occupied half the seats on the confederacy council. In 1640 the Attignawantan and the Attigneenongnahac (*Atingeennonniahak*), whose name meant Cord People or Cord-Making People (Steckley 1982b), claimed that they had formed the basis of the confederacy two hundred years previously. On formal occasions the members of these two groups called each other "brother" and "sister" and appear to have been accorded special ritual status as the founding members of the confederacy. The Arendahronon (*Arendaenronnon*), whose name may signify "Rock People," alluding to the fact that they had lived closer to the Canadian Shield than any other Huron group, joined the confederacy in the late sixteenth century; the Tahontaenrat (*Atahontaenrat*), or Deer People, joined still later. The Jesuits mention another group, the Ataronchronon (*Ataronchronnon*), or Swamp Dwellers, who lived east of the Attignawantan near the shores of Matchedash Bay. The Ataronchronon inhabited a number of small villages and may have been a division of the Attignawantan rather than a separate people. Although the Attignawantan was the largest Huron people, there were persistent disagreements and rivalry between its northern and southern branches. It is possible that the Ataronchronon was yet another division of this large but weakly integrated unit.

There are considerable difficulties in determining the geographical boundaries between these groups and the ethnic affiliations of some settlements. These problems are especially acute in the eastern part of the Huron country, which, because the Attignawantan tended to monopolize French visitors, was visited less frequently by Europeans.

Champlain states that there were eighteen settlements in the Huron country, Sagard says twenty-five (but this figure may include seven Tionontati ones), and the Jesuits report twenty. These differences may result from large communities dividing to form two or more small ones or a number of small villages joining together to form a single large settlement. The various figures may also reflect a difference of opinion about what constituted a settlement. The largest communities contained forty or more longhouses and each had a population of 1500–2000 people. There were about six of these large settlements in the Huron country, all of which were heavily fortified. In addition, there were smaller settlements, many of which were unfortified. The inhabitants of these villages fled to the large settlements in times of danger and attended council meetings and celebrations there as well. Thus, these villages were to some degree satellites of the larger communities. Some hamlets consisted of only one or two houses. In both cases there may have been differences of opinion about whether or not to count these as separate communities.

The Huron located their principal communities on slightly elevated ground adjoining a flowing stream. Settlements of the historical period tend to be found on natural eminences, such as hills, old shorelines, or meander spurs (Fig.3). They are also near good supplies of springwater and close to sandy, well-drained soil, which was favored for growing corn. The latter is found mostly on the sides and tops of hills rather than in the valley bottoms, which tended to be swampy. Many of the settlements that have been mapped in the Sturgeon Valley are located on fossil-lake terraces sixty meters or more above the present valley bottom, but near spots where springs flow from the sides of hills (Heidenreich 1967:17–18).

Settlements were not located directly on the shore of Georgian Bay because of poor soil conditions and to avoid the strong northwesterly winds that blew off the lake. Many of the Huron settlements were located near the streams flowing north into Georgian Bay. Because these streams were short and rose within the Huron country, they were useless to raiders from the south, but provided the Huron with excellent routes for traveling north to Lake Huron.

Fortified towns tended to be surrounded on two or three sides by natural depressions. The oval palisades that protected these communities were not constructed like those of a European fort, but consisted of cedar or pine poles 4.5 meters or more high and only 7–9 centimeters in diameter. The poles were sharpened at the base and were twisted into the ground a short distance apart. Usually there were three rows of stakes, one inside the other. These rows were woven together with smaller branches and reinforced between with large pieces of bark to form a solid barricade. The base of the palisade was further strengthened by piling earth against it or by pinning tree trunks to the ground lengthwise in front of it. Generally, the palisade was constructed most heavily where the settlement was most exposed to attack. Watchtowers and galleries were constructed on the inside of the wall and were reached by ladders made of notched logs. If an attack was expected, the galleries were stocked with rocks to hurl at the enemy and jars of water to put out fires. Usually a settlement had only one entrance. The two ends of the palisade were made to overlap in such a way that it was necessary for a person to turn at a right angle upon entering or leaving the community. The entrance passage was protected by bars rather than by a gate (Fig.4).

In 1636 the Attignawantan occupied fourteen settlements. Most of these were small and unfortified. The principal town was the large, palisaded community of Ossossané, located near the southern border of the Huron country. This town had approximately eight smaller settlements dependent on it. Farther north, in the Penetanguishene Peninsula, were five more settlements, which appear to have had the town of Angoutenc as their nucleus. At the time of Sagard's visit, Khinonascarant (*Ekhionnonhaskaren*) had been the

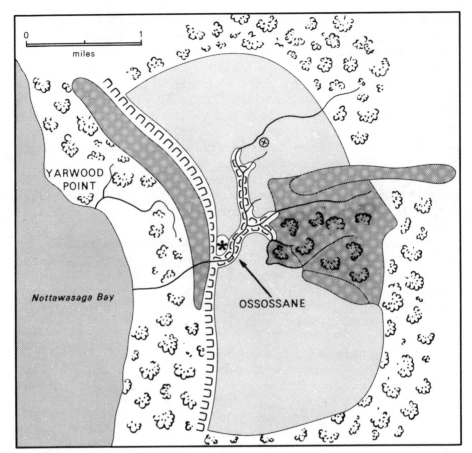

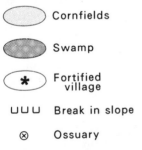

Figure 3. Reconstruction of field pattern and natural setting of Ossossané prior to 1634 (after C.E. Heidenreich 1971).

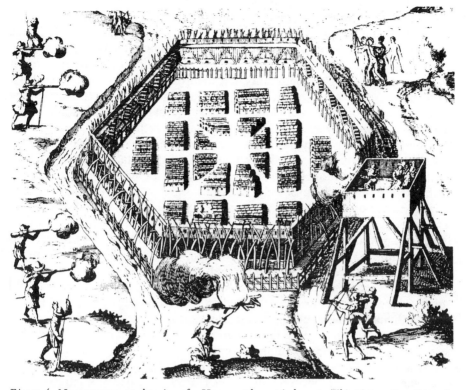

Figure 4. No contemporary drawing of a Huron settlement is known. This picture of an Iroquois town under attack by Champlain and his Huron allies in 1615 provides an idea of what a large Iroquoian settlement looked like to the French. Archaeological evidence indicates that both the open square and the regular layout of the houses are highly idealized.

main town in the north, but between 1623 and 1627 it had split into three small villages.

The settlements of the eastern Huron peoples were fewer in number but larger than those of the Attignawantan. Most of them were palisaded. The Tahontaenrat occupied a single large town, called Scanonerat (*Skannonaen-rat*). Unfortunately, it is not clear how many settlements belonged to each of the other two peoples or which ones they were. The Jesuit *Relation* of 1636 speaks of a confederacy council attended by the Attignawantan and two other tribes that had four settlements each. If the Tahontaenrat are here being counted as part of the Attigneenongnahac or Arendahronon, it is likely that the latter tribes shared seven communities between them.

One of the large Arendahronon settlements was Contarea (*Ekontareia*). It was located near Lake Couchiching and appears to have been the same community that the French called Saint Jean Baptiste (Heidenreich 1966:123–124). Another unnamed Arendahronon town, described as the "chief bulwark of the country," was destroyed by the Iroquois in 1642. Still a third may have been the community known to the French as Saint Joachim. It was located just east of the Sturgeon River. The important settlement of Taenhatentaron belonged either to the Arendahronon or to the Attigneenongnahac. It was located in the Sturgeon Valley not far south of Saint Joachim. Still farther south was Teanaostaiaé (*Teannaosteiai*). At the time of the Jesuit mission, it was said to be the largest community in the Huron country. It was the principal town of the Attigneenongnahac and the southernmost Huron settlement along the trail that led south to the Neutral country. West of it was Ekhiondatsaen, which was apparently also an Attigneenongnahac settlement.

Because so many Attignawantan communities were small ones, it is possible that this group contained less than half of the total population of the confederacy, even though it was the largest constituent people. From the point of view of Huron subsistence activities, small settlements had a number of advantages over large ones. Because less agricultural land was required, a settlement could remain in the same place longer without exhausting all the land and firewood within easy reach; hence, settlements had to be moved less often. If farming had been their only concern, the northern Iroquoians probably would have preferred to live in small communities.

Yet large settlements could defend themselves more easily than could small, scattered ones. Being protected from Iroquois attack by the Huron peoples living to the south and east, the northern Attignawantan had less need of large, fortified settlements than had other Huron groups. Nevertheless, the northern Attignawantan communities played a major role in the fur trade with the French, and there is no evidence that they were politically disadvantaged by comparison with larger Huron settlements. Ossossané, the largest Attignawantan community, was located on the exposed southern border of the Huron confederacy. When the Huron felt especially threatened by an Iroquois attack in 1635, five northern Attignawantan villages discussed building a single fortified town, a plan that was abandoned when the danger diminished. The three eastern peoples were much more exposed to Iroquois raiding parties, to the extent that warriors often had to stand guard while women worked in their fields. This is probably the reason why these peoples lived in a small number of large, well-fortified settlements. The distribution of the largest and most strongly fortified Huron settlements along the Hurons' exposed southern and eastern border suggests that defense, rather than the search for a more exciting life-style or the imposition of economic or political control over smaller neighboring communities, played a primary role in the establishment of larger settlements.

NEIGHBORING PEOPLES

The Iroquoian populations of the Lower Great Lakes region lived in clusters made up of a number of settlements; however, none of the other clusters was nearly as large as that formed by the coming together of the Huron confederacy. Between each of these clusters was forest land, which was used for hunting and fishing. Natural features served to demarcate the hunting territory that belonged to each group of settlements.

A short distance to the west of the Huron country, near the rugged part of the Niagara escarpment known as the Blue Mountain, lived the Tionontati (*Etionnontate*), or Mountain People, whom the French also referred to as the Petun or Tobacco Nation. Although the Tionontati were less numerous than the Huron, both groups spoke the same language and had similar customs. The Tionontati lived in seven to nine settlements, only two of which were of any size. Ehwae, their principal town, was burned by a hostile group, either the Assistaronon or the Iroquois, in 1640. They probably numbered 8000–9000.

Farther south in Ontario, from the Grand River Valley eastward across the Niagara River, was another Iroquoian confederacy that the French called the Neutral Nation, and the Huron the Atiwendaron. The latter was a term the Huron and Neutral applied to each other and which meant "people who speak a slightly different language." This implies that the Neutral language was less different from Huron than were the Iroquois languages. The Neutral confederacy was made up of several peoples, three or four of which are recorded on early maps. Their largest settlement clusters were located inland from the west end of Lake Ontario. Prior to 1639 the Wenro, an Iroquoian people who lived west of the Seneca in New York State, were associated with the Neutral. Following the severing of this alliance, the Wenro dispersed and some went to live with the Attignawantan.

Neutral customs differed from Huron ones in a number of ways. They are reported to have kept the bodies of the dead in their dwellings as long as possible; after the flesh had decayed they returned the bones to their houses, where they kept them until the Feast of the Dead was celebrated. The ossuaries, in which these bones were finally buried, were smaller than those of the Huron, and some groups buried their dead individually, as the Iroquois did. This suggests that burial was less an expression of community solidarity among the Neutral than among the Huron. Like the Tionontati, the Neutral were fond of tattooing their bodies, which were often covered all over with designs.

Wild fruits and nuts were plentiful in the Neutral country, which was warmer than that of the Huron. Game animals were also exceedingly abundant, and Neutral men were renowned for their skill as hunters. Archaeological evidence indicates that they depended more heavily on hunting and gathering to supply their subsistence needs than did the Huron (Ridley 1961). Their total population was larger than that of the Huron and they occupied forty communities, although most of these were villages and hamlets.

The Neutral were so named because they refused to become involved in warfare between the Huron and the Iroquois. Both groups were free to visit Neutral settlements and were forced to respect the peace there, although they might clash if they encountered each other unattended by Neutral in the intervening forests. The Neutral were at war with the Assistaronon (*Atsistaronnon*), a name that the Iroquoians who lived in Ontario gave to the

Algonkian-speaking peoples who inhabited what is now Michigan and Ohio, including the Kickapoo, Fox, and Mascouten. These groups, unlike the northern Algonkians, had a horticultural economy. The Assistaronon were also enemies of the Tionontati and appear to have controlled the eastern shore of Lake Huron south of the Bruce peninsula.

Most of the interior of southwestern Ontario was uninhabited and was used as hunting territory by the Neutral and Tionontati. Parts of it were too high and too cold to grow corn, and fish were not as abundant in the interior as they were nearer the Great Lakes. A number of Algonkian bands lived along the southern shores of Georgian Bay, others in the Bruce Peninsula. The best known of these groups were the Cheveux Relevés, or High Hairs, who dwelt west of the Tionontati, in the vicinity of the Beaver Valley. They grew some corn, but traveled extensively and relied on hunting and gathering to a greater extent than did the Iroquoians. In 1615 Champlain encountered three hundred of them drying blueberries near the northeastern corner of Georgian Bay. The Cheveux Relevés were part of a group of bands that later were known as the Ottawa.

The Huron were familiar with a number of peoples who lived south of the Great Lakes, all of them Iroquoian-speaking. The Mohawk, Oneida, Onondaga, Cayuga, and Seneca formed the Five Nations, or League of the Iroquois, a confederacy similar to that of the Huron. Each of the Iroquois peoples had one to three major settlements, as well as a number of smaller ones. Most of the larger communities were fortified. Champlain described the palisades surrounding the Iroquois town he attacked in 1615 as being stronger than those of any Huron settlement. Communities belonging to the same Iroquois people were located close to one another, but since each group built its settlements near the center of its hunting territory, the clusters of settlements belonging to different peoples were sixteen to sixty-five kilometers apart. Five of these clusters stretched across upper New York State between the Mohawk Valley and the Niagara frontier.

No reliable data are available concerning the population of the Iroquois confederacy. The ten or more large communities that they are recorded as occupying in the early seventeenth century do not suggest a smaller population than that of the Huron. The Iroquois, like the Huron, were stricken by serious epidemics of Old World diseases in the late 1630s and early 1640s, and afterwards they numbered about 12,000 (Snow and Starna 1989). It is likely that prior to this time they numbered 25,000–30,000. As a result of these epidemics, the Huron, Neutral, and Iroquois confederacies all appear to have lost over half their population. Further losses from war and disease may explain the failure of the Iroquois to increase after that time, in spite of the many captives they incorporated into their society beginning around 1640.

The Iroquois were the only peoples with whom the Huron were consistently at war in the seventeenth century. According to the Huron, they had been fighting for over fifty years. The nearest, most populous, and most feared of the Iroquois peoples were the Seneca.

Another Iroquoian group, known as the Erie or Cat (actually the Raccoon)

Nation, lived near the southeastern end of Lake Erie. Like their neighbors, the Erie were horticulturalists inhabiting a number of sedentary communities. The most southerly Iroquoian people with whom the Huron were in contact was the Andastoe or Susquehannock. They lived in the Susquehanna Valley, almost 1000 kilometers south of the Huron country. Like the Huron, the Susquehannock were at war with the Iroquois; hence the Huron and Susquehannock recognized each other as allies. Although the Iroquois tried to impede contact between these two groups, diplomatic missions as well as warriors seeking adventure secretly made their way through the intervening Iroquois territory. These warriors carried large amounts of wampum beads to the Huron. In 1647 a number of Susquehannock were reported to be living in the Huron country.

The territory north of the Huron country was entirely occupied by Algonkian-speaking peoples who subsisted mainly by hunting and fishing. Some of the groups that lived near Lake Nipissing and in the Ottawa Valley planted corn, but only in small amounts and as a supplement to their diet. Because of their subsistence pattern, the northern hunters were fewer in number, more dispersed, and less sedentary than were the peoples to the south, whether the latter were Algonkian or Iroquoian speaking.

All of these northern peoples had good relations with the Huron and obtained supplies of corn from them. The Huron were thoroughly familiar with the Algonkian bands that inhabited the shores of Georgian Bay, as well as with the Nipissing, an important group that had its headquarters near Lake Nipissing and traveled as far north as James Bay each summer, and with the various Algonkian bands that lived along the Ottawa River and its tributaries. The Huron were also in contact with Algonkian peoples who inhabited the southern interior of Quebec, perhaps as far east as Tadoussac. In addition, they visited the Upper Great Lakes, where they traded with various peoples including the Winnebago, a sedentary Siouan-speaking group that lived west of Lake Michigan.

TRAVEL

The native groups we have surveyed were those the Huron knew well and with whom they interacted. The extent of these contacts dispels any notion that the horticultural peoples of the Lower Great Lakes region were isolated from one another at this time. Although their contacts with the south were more limited than those with the north, the Huron knew more about what Dutch and English settlers were doing along the eastern seaboard of America than did the French who were living in Quebec.

The Huron normally traveled on foot within their own territory and when they visited the other peoples of southwestern Ontario. A network of trails linked the various Huron settlements. The main ones followed the ridges where the forests were less thick and there was less swampland than in the valleys. Beyond the Huron country, an important trail ran from Ossossané westward toward the Tionontati, while another went south from Teanaostaiaé to Kandoucho, the nearest Neutral town. Huron travelers along these routes usually carried with them only their bowl, spoon, and sleeping mat, since food and shelter were provided for them in the various towns they visited. In winter snowshoes were used to travel long distances and heavy loads were pulled on sledges.

When trading in the north, visiting their main fishing grounds, or making their way across Lake Ontario to attack the Iroquois, the Huron traveled by canoe. Among the nomadic peoples to the north, entire families traveled by canoe, but the Huron seem to have restricted this form of travel largely to men. Like the northern Algonkians, the Huron covered their canoes with birchbark. These canoes were lighter and swifter than those of the Iroquois and Neutral, which had to be made of elm or hickory bark since the canoe birch did not grow in their territories. Although easy to carry around portages, Huron canoes, which were up to six meters long and seventy-five centimeters wide, could hold from two to six people and over ninety kilograms of cargo. Small ones could be fashioned quickly when they were needed and were used for short trips, but large, carefully constructed canoes were preferred for long voyages. The main problem with canoes was that they were easily damaged and tended to leak. Because of this, Huron voyagers preferred to stay within sight of land.

The main water route to the north ran along the island-studded eastern shore of Georgian Bay, at the north end of which the Huron could turn either eastward through Lake Nipissing to the Ottawa Valley and Saint Lawrence River or westward following the north shore of Lake Huron towards Lake Superior and Michigan. Although fish and game were caught along the way, each Huron traveler carried a supply of cornmeal, as well as a clay pot used to bail out the canoe, cook meals, and urinate into without having to land. Each evening the boat was drawn up on the shore, and some men erected a rough birchbark shelter while others collected firewood and cooked the evening meal. Another meal was eaten in the morning before breaking camp. During the day the Huron did not stop to eat, although they frequently smoked to deaden their hunger. If a group planned to return along the same route, cornmeal carried in birchbark bags was deposited in caches at two-day intervals for the return journey. Travelers also erected signs painted on slabs of bark that recorded with pictograms the name of their home community and the number of men who were in each party.

3/The Huron Economy

In all northern Iroquoian societies a primary distinction was drawn, in religious beliefs as well as social life, between the clearing and the forest. The clearing, consisting of a settlement and its surrounding fields, was the realm where women lived in matrilineal extended families, raised their children, and grew the corn, beans, and squash that constituted the major basis of Iroquoian subsistence. Women and children rarely left this sheltered focus of Iroquoian society, and then only in the company of men. The forest, by contrast, was where men hunted, fished, traded, carried on diplomacy, waged war, and confronted the sometimes dangerous spirits inhabiting that realm.

This distinction constituted the central metaphor in terms of which relations between Iroquoian men and women were organized. Within the clearings, women's activities were the ones around which everyday life was organized, and women, especially older women, had a leading voice in making decisions about everything that related to the community. Men lived, almost as guests, in longhouses that were occupied, and largely provisioned, by two or more generations of women. The forest was the realm to which men could escape, if only temporarily, from the authority of women, while contributing to the support of their community.

Among the Huron everyday relations between adult men and women were characterized by a considerable amount of formality and avoidance. Huron men were anxious to assert their fortitude and resourcefulness, and to that end spent much time pursuing dangerous activities outside the community. Even within Huron settlements, life was organized in such a way that men and women spent much of every day apart from one another. In public they were formal and restrained in each other's presence, and in particular, a man was ashamed to be seen arguing with a woman. Nowhere, however, was the distinction between the sexes more evident than in the division of labor, specific tasks being considered appropriate for each sex. Young boys refused to perform women's tasks, such as carrying water, and men were subjected to public ridicule if necessity compelled them to cook food in the presence of a woman.

HORTICULTURE

In historical times Huron subsistence was predominantly based on horticulture. Crop yields accounted for perhaps three-quarters of all that was eaten. A striking feature of Huron food production, and of food production in the eastern woodlands generally, was the limited number of crops that were cultivated. Indian corn, beans, and squash were the three plants that were grown to be eaten. Corn was the most important crop, constituting the staple food of the Huron, but beans were of considerable nutritional importance and squash added variety to their diet. Sunflowers were grown for their seeds, from which oil was extracted which the Huron used to garnish food and rub on their bodies. Some tobacco was cultivated, although this plant grew better among the Tionontati and the Neutral, where the climate was milder. Because of the ability of native North American tobacco to produce altered states of consciousness, it was valued as a means of communicating with spirits and clearing the mind on ceremonial occasions as well as for deadening pain and hunger and as a source of social enjoyment. All the plants that the Huron grew were of southern origin; the sunflower being indigenous to the eastern United States, the rest to Mesoamerica. Considering the relatively short growing season in the Huron country and its location on the extreme northern limits of New World agriculture, it is not surprising that only a few of the most important and adaptable of Mesoamerican cultigens had made their way this far north.

The planting, care, and harvesting of crops were women's tasks. Only tobacco was grown by the men in small patches near their longhouses. Huron women worked the soil with small wooden spades (Fig.5). As a result, horticulture was restricted to light sandy loams of the sort that were common in the Huron country. Because these soils dried out easily, there was much anxiety about drought. Late spring frosts sometimes killed the seedlings and made it necessary to resow the fields, and in the summer the crops were threatened by insects. A serious drought occurred about one year in ten, and there were less severe problems with crops two or three times each decade (Heidenreich 1971:58–59). Because they feared famine, the Huron traditionally planted enough corn each spring to produce crops that could feed them for several years. Reports of famine following crop failures in the 1640s suggest that by this time most of their surplus production was being used in the fur trade. Crop failures often involved only a few communities, in which case any extra corn that was needed could be obtained from other parts of the country. If the failure was more prolonged and widespread, some Huron would go to live with their Neutral and Tionontati trading partners, while the rest relied on hunting and gathering. Because of their high population density, this could result in starvation and death for many Huron, who, after they had exhausted the wild plants that were normally eaten, were driven to consume mosses, tree bark, and lichen. This may account for some of the evidence of periodic malnutrition noted by physical anthropologists.

One of the most arduous horticultural tasks was the clearing of fields. The

Figure 5. Huron women growing corn. From Joseph François Lafitau, Moeurs des sauvages, *1724.*

transformation of forest into clearing was men's work; like hunting, fishing, and waging war, it preserved the life of the community by inflicting death on other living things, in this case upon trees. Armed with stone axes, the men cut down the smaller trees, some of which were used for construction purposes, then girdled the larger ones and stripped off some of their branches. After they were sufficiently dry, these branches were burned at the base of the larger trees to kill them. The women then planted their crops between the stumps. The stumps were removed only when they became rotten and could be broken up easily. This was slow work, and prior to the introduction of iron axes, the clearing of new fields had to begin several years before they were needed. It was also an unremitting task, since Huron horticultural practices forced them to relocate their settlements at intervals which varied between ten and thirty years; larger settlements perhaps having to be resettled more frequently than small ones. This was necessary because annual cropping soon depleted the fertility of the soil, and the clearing of new fields around a settlement exhausted nearby supplies of wood suitable for fires and building houses. It is estimated that the natural fertility of the types of soil the Huron cultivated was sufficient to grow crops for only four to six years; however, by burning dried cornstalks to add ash to the soil and carefully weeding their fields, Huron women were able to keep them productive for eight to twelve years (Heidenreich 1971:180–189). Unless threatened with extermination, Iroquoians rarely moved their communities more than a few kilometers at a time. This made it easier for men to clear fields in a new location prior to the actual move. When a longer move became necessary, those involved would try to settle near an existing settlement, where they might obtain provisions and borrow fields in which they could grow crops for the first few years. A move into virgin territory could spell disaster for any large group.

It is not known precisely how much land in the Huron country was under cultivation at any one time. On the basis of his observation of traditional subsistence activities on Iroquois reservations in New York State, William Fenton believes that 2833 hectares would have been enough to support a population of 20,000 (Pendergast and Trigger 1972:8,n.6). This agrees closely with Heidenreich's (1971:213) estimate that a settlement with 1000 inhabitants would have required at least 146 hectares of arable land to support itself. In spite of extensive cornfields and abandoned clearings not yet grown over with new trees, there were still extensive tracts of forest within the heart of the historical Huron country. Moreover, there is no evidence that particular locales were being reinhabited at regular intervals. Even in the Huron country, the pressure on land does not appear to have been great enough to induce particular communities to occupy a number of specified sites in rotation.

Teams of men working together could clear as much land as they wanted or were able, and this land remained in the possession of their extended families as long as the women of these families wished to cultivate it. Once abandoned, however, a field could be used by anyone who wished to do so. It is unclear to what degree each woman regarded the corn, beans, and squash she planted as her own property, or the women living in a single longhouse considered all the food they produced to be their collective possession. The large vats or casks used to store most of the corn were located in the porches at the ends of longhouses, not in the sections belonging to individual nuclear families. The reciprocity and sharing among the women who occupied a single longhouse must have encouraged the *de facto* pooling of resources, particularly if some women were too old or ill to produce their own food. The older women of each longhouse played a leading role in organizing the planting and harvesting of crops.

Each May, which was called "planting time" in the Huron calendar (Steckley 1983), the women carefully cleaned their fields and prepared their corn for planting by selecting the best kernels from last year's surplus and soaking them in water for several days. Nine or ten kernels were then planted in each cornhill. These cornhills, which were used year after year, were low hillocks of soft earth that the women had scraped together. The remains of fields dotted with these cornhills, each somewhat under a meter in diameter and located about a meter apart, were still visible when northern Simcoe County and other parts of southern Ontario were resettled during the nineteenth century. The cornhills were arranged in no particular order, no doubt initially to avoid the many tree trunks that remained standing. Later, as the trunks were removed, their density increased to 6200 hills per hectare. The hills not

Figure 6. Huron women living in a small cabin in the fields during the summer. One pounds corn, while two others fetch firewood and water. From Novae Franciae Accurata Delineatio.

only helped to support the cornstalks but also prevented sheet erosion and, by trapping cold, low-lying air between them, reduced the danger of frost damage to the plants (Heidenreich 1974). Huron women grew their corn, beans, and squash in the same fields, using cornstalks as poles to support the bean plants. To avoid the danger of late frosts, they planted their squash seed in bark trays filled with powdered wood, which they kept near the fires in their longhouses. After the seeds had sprouted, the young plants were transferred to the fields. Huron women brought much detailed technical knowledge to their growing of crops.

In parts of the country that were sheltered from enemy raiders, the women often left the villages during the early summer and went with their children to live in cabins near their fields (Fig.6). These were smaller versions of Huron longhouses, each belonging to a single extended family. During the summer the women took great care to keep their fields clean of weeds, while the children chased away birds and small animals. The corn, most of which belonged to the Northern Flint variety, grew almost two meters high, matured in just over three months, and bore two or three ears, each yielding between 100 and 650 kernels. When the corn was harvested, in early September, the leaves were pulled back and the cobs tied in bundles that were hung from poles under the roofs of the longhouses. When the kernels were dry and fit for storage the women shelled and cleaned them, then stored them in large vats. Young corn was preserved by picking the cobs before they were ripe and roasting them. Sliced and dried squash remained edible for up to five months.

Because the Huron feared drought and frost, they sought supernatural protection against such disasters. Certain shamans claimed to be able to control the weather. Some would predict frost, suggesting at the same time that it could be prevented if the Huron burned a little tobacco each day in their fields to honor the sky. In times of drought others would promise to produce rain in return for public gifts. Under their direction rituals were performed to end the drought. If these rituals were not successful, the shaman sought to protect his reputation by attributing his failures to sorcery or other malign influences. If he experienced a series of failures, people lost faith in him.

COLLECTING

In addition to caring for crops, women gathered a wide variety of wild plants, which added flavor and variety to an otherwise bland diet. Berries of many kinds were collected, and some were dried for winter use, as treats for the sick, to flavor corn soup, and to put into small cakes that were baked in ashes. Acorns, walnuts, and grapes were commonly eaten. The Jerusalem artichoke (*Helianthus tuberosus*), a wild relative of the sunflower, was rare in the Huron country but its tubers were eaten, either raw or cooked, as was *sondhratates* (*sandratathes*) (possibly ground nut, *Apios americana*, or cow parsnip, *Heracleum lanatum*). Ripe chives were baked in ashes. Some plants required special treatment before they were edible. Plums were bitter prior to being touched by the frost unless they were buried in the ground before being eaten. Acorns were boiled several times to take away their bitter taste.

The women also gathered and split all the wood that was needed for cooking and heating the houses. Dry wood was preferred because it produced less smoke. They did not collect twigs or the trunks of large trees, which were left to rot because the Huron lacked the means to cut them up. The best wood was available after the winter storms had knocked the dead limbs from trees. During two days in March or April, the women from each settlement helped one another collect all the wood that was needed for the following year. This wood was tied in faggots, which the women carried back to the village on tumplines. If a girl married at a time of year when wood was difficult to obtain, the women of her community gave her some of their own as a present. The firewood was stored in the porches and living quarters of long-houses.

Another communal activity was the gathering of Indian hemp (*Apocynum cannabinum*), a plant that grew in marshy places and from which rope was made. If there was danger of enemy attack, some warriors would accompany the women and might help them gather the hemp. Rope was also made from shredded and boiled basswood bark.

HUNTING AND FISHING

Fishing, which was of major importance for Huron subsistence, was mainly a male activity. Much of it was done with a wooden spear to which a barbed head whittled and ground out of bone was attached. Numerous examples of these "harpoon heads" have been found in archaeological sites; they have several barbs along one side and a perforation near the lower end. Even more fishing was done with nets made of Indian hemp rope. Net fishing was done both on the open water and at openings in weirs, where baskets were also used. The most important set of Huron weirs was built at the Narrows between Lakes Simcoe and Couchiching. The Huron also fished with hook and line, the hook being made of wood with a bone barb attached, but since the lines were weak, this approach was not particularly effective.

Various kinds of fish were caught in different places and at different seasons of the year. The most important fishing expeditions were those made in October and early November to the many islands in Georgian Bay to catch *atsihiendo*, which is generally identified as whitefish but which linguistic evidence suggests was lake trout (Steckley 1986a). Each fishing party had its own leader and erected a bark cabin on the island it selected to be its base of operations. These were built in the Algonkian fashion: a typical cabin containing two fireplaces and sheltering four groups of closely related kinsmen in each corner. Each evening, unless the lake was too choppy, the Huron set their nets over a kilometer from the island and drew them in again at daybreak. They immediately gutted the fish they caught. If the weather was good, the fish were spread on racks made of wooden poles to dry; if not, they were smoked and packed in bark containers. Some of the fish were boiled to extract oil from them. This oil was stored in gourd containers and used to garnish food during the winter. If a number of fishing cabins were erected close together, the men of each took turns feasting and entertaining each other in the evenings.

A few weeks after the *atsihiendo* season ended, the Huron went to catch *einchataon* (*annentrataon*), possibly the burbot or "freshwater cod," which was used to flavor corn soup. This fish, which was caught with a net cast from the shore, was not gutted but was hung in bunches beneath the roofs of longhouses, where it remained edible throughout the winter. The liver of the burbot is especially rich in vitamins A and D (Steckley 1986a). At other times of the year large schools of lake herring (*auhaitsiq* [*awatsik*]) were taken in nets. Entire communities cooperated in catching these fish, each person carrying away his or her share in large wooden bowls. Some of these fish were eaten fresh; the rest were smoked. In the winter, fish were taken through the ice. This was done with a net passed by means of a pole from one hole to another, the holes being arranged in a circular fashion.

Hunting was considerably less important from a nutritional point of view, although animal skins were necessary for making clothing (Gramly 1977). It was also an activity that Huron men greatly enjoyed. Birds, such as geese and the great blue heron, were stalked with bow and arrow or were caught with nets. Often this was done in the fields, where large numbers of them gathered when the corn was ripe. Some birds, such as crows, were not eaten. Wild turkeys were common in certain areas, particularly southwest of the Huron settlements in the direction of the Tionontati.

Because of the demands of so large a population, most game animals were hunted-out in the regions adjacent to Huron settlement, even though their abandoned cornfields would have provided ideal conditions for the multiplication of deer. As a result, meat was scarce or unobtainable during much of the year, and skins for clothing often were in short supply. Hunting expeditions had to travel a considerable distance south and east of the Huron country in order to find game. Most hunting occurred in the fall, with the hunters staying away for a month or more before returning to their settlements in time for the winter religious festivals. War parties returning from the Iroquois country also hunted in the area north of Lake Ontario. In late winter, hunting parties made up of several hundred people journeyed for several days beyond the borders of the Huron country. Women are reported to have gone along on some of these winter expeditions, probably to help butcher the game and carry home the skins and meat. They do not appear to have joined the autumn hunts, possibly because enemy raiders were still active at that time of year.

The principal game animal, and the one the Huron men most enjoyed hunting, was deer. These were pursued in drives, which required the cooperation of large numbers of men. Sometimes several hundred hunters would land on a large island or form a line through the forest between one bend in the river and the next. Then, making a loud noise, they would drive the animals toward a fixed point along the water. As the deer sought to pass through the line into the water, they were either shot with arrows or killed with sharpened poles by men standing in canoes. On other occasions, the hunters built a triangular enclosure in the forest, open on one side but enclosed along the other two with barriers of brush up to three meters high. The sides of these enclosures were over a kilometer long, and at the narrow end they led the deer into a pen from which they were unable to escape (Fig.7). Twenty-five men could construct such an enclosure within less than ten days. When it was finished, the hunters lined up before dawn at the open end and, beating sticks together, drove the deer into the pen at the narrow end, where they killed them with arrows. Repeating this activity every second day for thirty-eight days, one band of hunters was able to kill 120 deer. The skins and fat of these animals were carefully preserved, but only a little of the meat was carried back to the Huron country to be used in feasts. The main objective of these hunts was to obtain large skins for clothing. The cold weather was useful because it preserved the meat and allowed the hunters to haul the skins back to their settlements on sleds.

The other important game animals were beaver and bears. Bears were tracked with specially trained dogs, then shot with arrows (Fig.8). The meat was preserved for feasts and the bears' entrails were fed to the dogs as a reward. Killing a bear sometimes required tackling the animal at dangerously close range, and various medical remedies were prescribed specifically for bear bites. Beaver were usually hunted in the winter, since they remained in their lodges at that season and their pelts were of better quality than in the summer. A hole was chopped through the roofs of their houses and they were killed at holes cut in the ice when they had to surface to breathe. In the summer beaver were sometimes caught in nets. Beaver meat was eaten by the Huron, either fresh or smoked, and even before the beginning of the fur

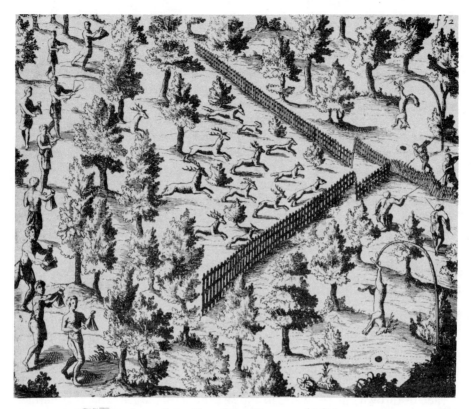

Figure 7. A Huron deer hunt. From Champlain's Voyages *of 1619.*

trade their skins were valued for clothing and sewn together to make robes. The incisor teeth were used as woodworking tools. Muskrats as well as beaver were hunted by the Huron. The Huron also took a wide variety of smaller animals. Rabbits were caught in snares and tortoises were collected and eaten. A large-sized variety of mouse which infested the settlements was also consumed.

Hunting and fishing were the focus of many ritual activities designed to protect the person involved and bring him luck. Hunters frequently sought the advice of shamans or guardian spirits before starting out. Some fasted for a week or more and cut themselves so that their blood flowed profusely. The latter was done as an auto-sacrifice to invoke the aid of a man's guardian spirit and other spirits associated with the chase. While they were hunting and fishing, the Huron were careful not to burn the bones of any fish or animals or to let the fat of animals drop into the fire. They were also careful not to throw the bones of animals to the dogs. They feared that the souls of the animals they killed might report such maltreatment to living animals, who as a consequence would not permit themselves to be taken. They also believed that fish did not like the dead; hence, they were careful to keep their nets

Figure 8. A lone hunter pursuing game. From Novae Franciae Accurata Delineatio.

out of sight of human corpses and did not go fishing when one of their friends or relatives had died.

When strong winds prevented the Huron from setting their nets, they would observe various rituals to assure good fishing. Tobacco sometimes was burned or thrown into the water to appease the spirits. Each cabin of fishermen on the islands in Georgian Bay had a "fish preacher," who was believed to be endowed with special powers to speak to the fish and attract them into their nets. Men thought to possess such powers were highly esteemed. One shaman announced that, in order to assure large catches of fish, the Huron should give him presents and that at the start of the fishing season and while it lasted those planning to fish should burn tobacco in their fires in honor of his guardian spirit. People in many settlements complied, and fishing was good that year. The Huron also noted that two of the principal chiefs of a community that did not send the shaman presents were drowned on Georgian Bay during a thunderstorm while returning from fishing.

Huron men also relied on charms to make them lucky in hunting, fishing, trading, fighting, gambling, and amorous adventures. Some charms had the power to confer many benefits; others were useful for only one purpose. Charms were highly valued and were inherited from one generation to the next. In some cases a new charm was revealed to a man in a dream. If a hunter found an animal difficult to kill and later discovered something unusual in its entrails, such as a stone or a dead snake, he would keep what he found in the hope that it would bring him good luck. Likewise, stones that had a curious shape were collected, since it was believed that they might have belonged to a spirit who lived in the woods and had lost them. These included old projectile points that were of different shapes from those currently being manufactured. Some charms were obtained in trade from neighboring peoples, especially from the northern Algonkians, who were believed to possess especially powerful ones because they were renowned as hunters and fishermen. These charms were the most expensive merchandise in the region. Men carried their charms about with them in their pouches. From time to time they spoke to them and would offer them a few beads or a bit of tobacco as a present. They also gave feasts to make their charms more powerful and invoked their aid with special songs.

The Hurons stated that some of their hunting and fishing customs were of Algonkian origin. Among these was a ceremony in which two girls who had not yet reached puberty were married for the coming year to the spirit of a fishing net. This ceremony, which was said to ensure good fishing, was reported to have begun among the Algonkians when the spirit of a net appeared to a man in a dream asking for a bride to replace the wife he had lost. The ceremony then spread to the Huron. In return for consenting to the marriage, the girls' families were given a special share of the season's catch. While some hunting and fishing customs were of Algonkian origin, many others were probably survivals from the not too remote period when hunting and fishing were much more important to Huron subsistence than they were in the historical period. While these protective rituals may reflect the dangers involved in hunting and fishing, they also may have been partly an attempt to stress the importance of male activities, by emphasizing the rituals that surrounded them.

TAME ANIMALS

The Huron kept large numbers of dogs, who lived with them in their houses. These dogs were given names and permitted to eat at will out of the cooking pots. The women also let puppies suck food from their mouths in the same way that young children did. Some dogs were used for hunting, and dog meat was in special demand at feasts. Dogs were often sacrificed and eaten in Huron rituals, where they served as substitutes for human victims. Other dogs were so much loved by their owners that they would not permit them to be killed or sacrificed. A man who especially loved a particular dog transferred its name to a younger one when it died, just as human names were passed from the dead to the living. Bears were also used for sacrifice. These were usually young animals captured after their mothers had been killed by hunters. Such bears were given names and kept for several years in small, round enclosures within longhouses, where they were fed with leftovers from the meals. Some people kept tame birds either as pets or for eating, but this practice was not common.

MANUFACTURING

In spite of the Hurons' large numbers and their interest in intergroup trade, their economy was focused mainly at the level of the household. Because they had to relocate their settlements at relatively frequent intervals, they did not seek to accumulate large amounts of furniture or invest time in creating large and ornate possessions. Household furnishings tended to be portable or easily replaceable. Few, if any, distinctions were drawn between the manufacturing of goods for household use and for exchange. There were no full-time craft specialists, every able-bodied adult being expected to engage in food production. Each household, consisting of a number of nuclear families, manufactured all of its own basic needs. As with food production, clear distinctions were drawn between men's and women's tasks.

In addition to cooking and tending to other household chores, the women ground their surplus corn into meal, which was traded for meat and skins with the northern Algonkians. Women wove mats out of reeds and corn leaves, which they used to cover the doors and sleeping platforms of their houses. These mats were apparently not colored, as were those of the Algonkians. Women also fashioned baskets out of reeds and birchbark and sewed together birchbark eating and drinking bowls. They made fiber from the Indian hemp they collected and rolled it into twine on their thighs. The men used this twine to manufacture snares and fishing nets, a task performed during the winter months. Textile work that was produced by women included scarfs, collars, and bracelets, which were worn by both men and women. Samples with a twisted weave have been recovered archaeologically. Women also scraped and softened animal skins using small chert or bone scrapers. From these and from skins obtained from the northern Algonkians, Huron women made clothes, game bags, and tobacco pouches. The sewing was done with bone awls and pieces of sinew. Huron clothing offered considerable protection against the rain and the cold. Yet some Huron froze to death every winter while traveling between settlements. The fact that the Huron sought to obtain clothing, as well as skins, from the northern Algonkians suggests that these hunting peoples were able to manufacture garments that were better constructed and warmer than those made by the Huron.

The women also fashioned the globular pottery vessels that were used for cooking, storing food, and transporting water. To produce these vessels, clay was dried and pulverized, then mixed with a little powdered metamorphic rock to reduce the danger of cracking as the vessel dried. Water was added and the clay shaped into a ball. A hole was made in the ball with a fist and enlarged with the help of a wooden paddle to form the thin globular body of the pot. A constricted neck was added as well as a low rim that sometimes had V-shaped projections which made pouring easier. The pot was then dried in the sun and baked over an open fire. Archaeological evidence indicates that pottery vessels were manufactured in most, if not all, households, although it is not known if each adult woman made her own, or one or two

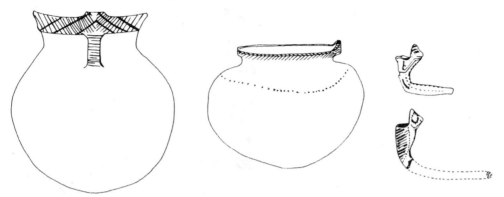

Figure 9. Huron pottery. Left: two Huron pots. Right: two effigy pipes.

women in each extended family produced all the pots needed by its members.

Ceramic pots ranged in size from tiny vessels to ones that were almost a meter in diameter. Cooking vessels were made in three size ranges intended for use by individuals, families, and for public feasts. Decoration was mostly confined to the lip and consisted of simple patterns composed of incised horizontal, vertical, and oblique lines (Fig.9). Archaeologists assign most of the pots from historical Huron sites to three types, which differ primarily in the shape of the lip and the pattern of incised decoration (MacNeish 1952). Regardless of use, Huron pottery had only one basic shape. This contrasts with the numerous forms of pottery vessels found in cultures of that period in the southeastern United States. Although Huron pots could be set directly over a fire, when cold they could not hold water for a long time without becoming soft and friable.

Smoking pipes were also made out of clay, which was normally shaped around a grass core that burned away when the pipe was fired. Pipes were generally better made than pottery vessels, the clay being more carefully selected and evenly fired. Some pipes were given a blackened surface by rubbing grease on them prior to firing (Kidd 1949:149). In addition to pipes with round and flaring bowls, the Huron manufactured a wide range of pipes decorated with human and animal figures. When Pierre Boucher (1664:101) stated that men made the pipes, he was probably referring to ones made of clay as well as stone. The finest pipes were the work of talented potters, and a small number of people must have produced them. Pipes were exchanged over wide areas. This may explain why they frequently were treasured, and, when broken, were glued together with blood their owner drew from his arm to use as an adhesive.

During the warmer months, when they could work out of doors, men built houses and constructed palisades around their towns. These labors, like the clearing of agricultural land, were part of the transformation of forest into clearing—a male activity that created a realm judged to be suitable for women and children to inhabit. Men also fashioned canoes at this time. Most of this

Figure 10. Carved bone human figure from historic Huron site. Length: nine centimeters.

work was done by teams made up of relatives, friends, or all the able-bodied men of a community.

Winter was not a time of leisure, but a season when work went on indoors. Men wove fishing nets and made bows and arrows, snowshoes, sleds, clubs, and suits of armor. They also carved wooden bowls, spoons, and ladles. The latter were sometimes fashioned out of antler in the shape of a duck in flight. They chipped and ground chisels and rectangular axes and adzes out of hard stones such as diorite and granite, but rarely bothered to give these utilitarian items a careful finish. Scrapers and drills were made from imported chert, or, when that was not available, from quartzite pebbles recovered from the glacial till. Small triangular projectile points were chipped out of chert or made from bone, which was also used to make harpoon points as well as various forms of awls and needles.

Men also manufactured a variety of ornamental objects. They transformed bird bones into tubular beads and fashioned discoidal ones from the ribs of marine shells. Long beads that were square in cross-section, as well as ones in the shape of turtles and other animals were ground from red slate, although these may have been obtained from the Ottawa rather than made by the Huron themselves (Fox 1980). Pipes, occasionally with effigy bowls, were carved out of stone, and combs and small amulets, some in human form, were whittled from bone (Fig.10).

FOREIGN TRADE

The key role that the Huron played in the French fur trade was an extension of their role as traders, which had begun in prehistoric times. By the seventeenth century, trade had become not only a source of luxury goods and a means of cementing alliances with neighboring peoples but also a source of skins and meat that were vital to a dense population that had outstripped the resources of its nearby hunting territories.

Chronic hostility between the Huron and the Iroquois confederacies made trade between them impossible. Occasionally, however, when there were negotiations between these two groups, the Huron chiefs gave their Iroquois counterparts presents of beaver skins and in return received wampum beads, which came from Long Island and the Chesapeake Bay area. In the seventeenth century, the Huron traded with the other Iroquoian peoples of Ontario. Although the Neutral obtained a certain amount of European trade goods from the Iroquois, and possibly also from the Susquehannock, the Huron maintained a nearly total monopoly over the trade goods that were entering Ontario from the Saint Lawrence Valley. While the Tionontati obtained some European goods from their Ottawa trading partners, the Ottawa got them from the Huron either directly or through the Nipissing. The desire of the Tionontati and Neutral to obtain iron axes, metal kettles, and glass beads seems to have brought their former conflicts with the Huron to an end and promoted increasing trade and friendship among the various Iroquoian peoples of southern Ontario.

Most of the goods that the Huron sought to obtain from these other Iroquoian groups were luxury items. One of their most valued imports was tobacco, which grew better among the Tionontati and the Neutral than it did in the Huron country. The Huron obtained large numbers of black squirrel skins from the Neutral, from which they made cloaks which they and their Algonkian trading partners greatly prized. From the Neutral they also received raccoon-skin robes, which came from the Erie country, and marine shells which ultimately came from the Chesapeake Bay region. The bulk of these shells were lightning whelk (*Busycon sinistrum*) and snow whelk (*Busycon laeostomum*) (Pendergast 1989). These shells were used to make beads. The Huron also stored some of their oil in gourds that came from the south.

A small amount of the goods that the Huron obtained from the northern Algonkians fell into the category of luxury items. These included winter clothing, often elaborately embroidered with porcupine quills, camping equipment, various kinds of charms, buffalo robes, which came from west of Sault Sainte Marie, and native copper from the mines on Lake Superior. In return, these Algonkians received tobacco and robes made of black squirrel and raccoon skins.

The bulk of the trade with the north was in more basic items. To the northern hunters, the Huron country was a source of cornmeal, which helped them to stay alive over the harsh winters. Hunter-gatherers, such as the Nipissing and the Ottawa Valley Algonkian, wintered each year in the Huron country. In mid-autumn they began to move toward the Huron, carrying the furs they had trapped themselves or collected from more remote bands over the summer. On the way they stopped to fish on Georgian Bay, drying as many fish as possible, both for their own use and to exchange with the Huron. When they reached the Huron country, they set up their winter camps near Huron settlements. The Arendahronon appear to have been on particularly good terms with one of the Algonkian bands from the Ottawa Valley, with whom their warriors were happy to travel and to fight alongside. It is probably because of this special relationship that the Arendahronon were the first Huron people to encounter the French on the Saint Lawrence. The Nipissing wintered farther west, among the Ataronchronon or Attignawantan.

The Huron did not bother to learn the languages of their neighbors, while their own language was a *lingua franca* among the Assistaronon and other Algonkian-speaking peoples with whom they traded. The language situation, which reflected the key role that the Huron played in the trading networks around the Upper Great Lakes, confirmed the Huron in their belief that they were more intelligent than any of their neighbors. Even French traders were expected to use the Huron language. The Attignawantan were especially high-handed in their political dealings with the Ottawa Valley Algonkian, possibly because they resented their alliance with the Arendahronon.

In addition to the trade that was carried on within the Huron country, each summer Huron traders traveled north along the water routes of Lake Huron to visit the Algonkians. These trips took groups of traders as far west as Lakes Superior and Michigan and eastward into central Quebec. In the winter the Huron crossed the ice of Georgian Bay to trade cornmeal for fish with nearby bands (Fig. 11).

There is good evidence that the Huron traded with the northern hunters long before the arrival of the Europeans. While most of the goods that were exchanged are perishable and therefore difficult to trace in the archaeological record, Ontario Iroquoian pottery dating as early as A.D. 1000 has been found in numerous Algonkian sites in northern Ontario. One of these is the stratified site at Frank Bay, which is a Nipissing encampment, but, were it not for the stone tools and some of the pottery, might be considered Huron (Ridley 1954). Beginning around A.D. 1200, strong Ontario Iroquoian influences can be seen in the pottery, house types, and burial practices at the Juntunen site in the Straits of Mackinac (McPherron 1967).

Trade was governed by elaborate rules. The rights to trade along a particular route belonged to the family or clan segment of the man who first discovered it. No one was supposed to trade along that route without receiving permission from the spokesman of the group that controlled it, which was normally granted only in return for presents. If a man engaged in trade without permission, the owner of the route and his supporters had the right, if they were strong enough, to attack him and despoil him of his goods as he returned home. Once he was safely back in his settlement, however, they could only complain about his behavior.

The men who went trading did so for both profit and adventure. Traveling among foreign peoples was a dangerous activity and served to test a man's courage. It also provided men with opportunities to enjoy themselves in various activities, such as gambling with their trading partners.

Although most of the trading was done by men in the prime of life, the major trade routes were under the control of important chiefs. At the time of Sagard's visit, men from neighboring settlements came to Khinonascarant

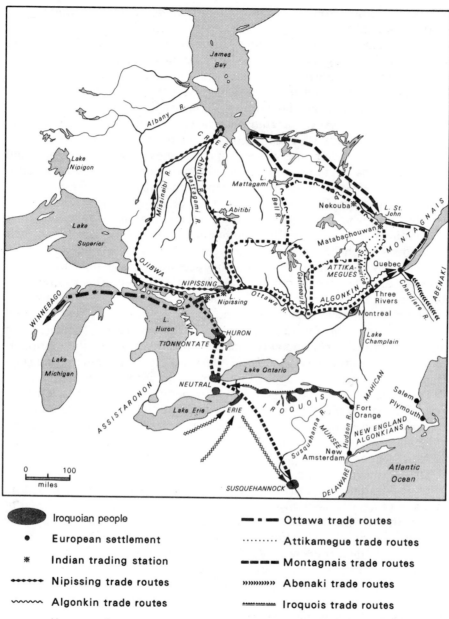

Figure 11. Major Indian trade routes in the first half of the seventeenth century.

to seek permission from chief Onorotandi (*Onnonrotandi?*) to trade along the rivers and lakes leading to the Saguenay and from his brother Awendaon to go to Quebec. Because the first Huron to encounter the French were Arendahronon, this group theoretically could have claimed the privilege of being the only Huron who could trade with the French. Because they knew that they could not defend this claim against the more powerful Attignawantan and wished to maintain good relations with the rest of the Huron confederacy, their principal chief, Atironta (*Hatironta*), agreed to share his people's trading privileges with the chiefs of the three other Huron peoples.

Control over trade routes was an important means by which a man could obtain wealth he might use to increase his reputation within Huron society. Yet lucrative new trade routes seem inevitably to have come under the control of hereditary chiefs, thereby enhancing their prestige. Ordinary traders, especially those who pioneered new trade routes, may have enhanced their reputation and influence, but they do not appear to have sought to use their trade goods to challenge the position of hereditary officeholders. On the contrary, they sought to use the wealth they acquired through trade to enhance the status of the local clan group to which they belonged. This was done by putting much of this wealth at the disposal of clan chiefs to give away in traditional distributive rituals. With the expansion of activity that followed the introduction of the fur trade, the ability of traditional chiefs to redistribute wealth was probably considerably enhanced. This may explain the sobriquets *hatirontas* (?), *hatiwannens*, and *hondakhienhai* (big stones, elders, and stay-at-homes) that were being applied to them in the historical period.

The chiefs attempted to regulate the number of young men who left their settlements at any one time to trade. They did this by spreading rumors that Iroquois attacks were expected. This required a sufficient number of warriors to remain in each town over the summer to protect the women, children, and old men from enemy war parties.

The Huron also tried hard to eliminate competition from foreign traders. Only a few Europeans, such as Etienne Brûlé who had lived among the Huron for many years, sufficiently won the Hurons' trust that they were allowed to travel with them into the far north. Even after the Huron concluded a treaty of friendship with the Tionontati, around 1640, they refused to let the Tionontati share in their trade with the French. This clearly demonstrates that the Huron confederacy was not merely a grouping of independent peoples who had agreed not to wage war against one another, as the Iroquois confederacy appears to have been at that time. The Huron confederacy was also a grouping of peoples who were willing to share in the same general trade and to protect this trade from outsiders. This reinforces the contention that trade had played an important role in molding the historical Huron settlement pattern.

The Huron valued their trade, both as a source of exotic and useful goods and as a means of cultivating friendly relations with neighboring peoples. To preserve it they had to conform to age-old conventions that were understood and accepted by all the peoples of the region. Trading was embedded in a complex network of social relations, and the exchange of goods occurred in the form of reciprocal gift giving. The Huron regarded reciprocity as an integral part of any kind of friendly or cooperative interaction, and ties between trading partners were viewed as similar in kind to those that bound relatives together. Visits to foreign trading partners were an occasion for several days of feasting, speech making, and the formal exchange of gifts. Before entering a village, the Huron traders would stop to paint their faces and put on their best clothes and ornaments. During an initial round of speeches, they gave the local chiefs valuable presents and asked them to ensure that in the exchanges that followed the Huron would receive the best quality goods at reasonable prices. After the individual exchanges were over, there was a further round of feasting and ceremonies, in the course of which the chiefs of the host community gave the Huron presents that were equal in value to those they had received at the beginning of the visit. Before leaving, the Huron were invited to return the next year. Even in dealing with the Neutral and Tionontati, with whom less formal individual trading occurred, visits between chiefs maintained the alliance and set the rates of exchange which were a precedent for individual trade.

The French recognized that the Huron were skillful traders and admired the manner in which they procured furs from native groups throughout large areas of northern Ontario and southwestern Quebec. Yet they noted that the Huron refused to haggle over the price of individual items and became annoyed if the French tried to do so. While Huron traders gave every indication of understanding market behavior, they never openly expressed a profit motive. Fluctuating rates of exchange mirrored the changing availability or demand for particular goods, but higher or lower exchange rates were invariably requested as proof of friendship and a means of reinforcing alliances between different peoples. Huron success in trade depended largely on their skills in maintaining good relations with foreign groups, and in particular with the northern Algonkians who had economies that were complementary to their own. This was done by extending hospitality to these peoples, by gift giving, and by the careful observation of protocol. By the early seventeenth century, the Huron had created a set of trading alliances that embraced all nearby groups except the Iroquois.

There was always the danger that if a Huron and someone from a friendly trading group got into a brawl and one of them was killed, this would lead to a war which would disrupt trade between the two groups. Such crises were even more serious because of the difficulty of finding someone to mediate them. It was, therefore, a Huron custom to pay more gifts to compensate for a murder of this sort than for the murder of one Huron by another. Champlain describes in detail a quarrel that broke out between the Huron and some Ottawa Valley Algonkian who were wintering near the Arendahronon town of Cahiagué (*Kahiaye*). The quarrel arose when the leading Algonkian chief decided to spare the life of an Iroquois prisoner whom the Huron had given him and instead of torturing the prisoner had adopted him. The Huron, angered by this, sent one of their warriors to the Algonkian camp to kill the Iroquois. The Algonkians retaliated by killing the Huron, whereupon the men of Cahiagué took up arms and attacked the Algonkian camp, wounding the chief and pillaging the cabins. At this point, Champlain was called upon to be an arbitrator. He managed, after intricate negotiations, to settle this conflict, being aided to no small degree by the desire of both parties to maintain their trading alliance.

The Huron sometimes exchanged children with their foreign trading partners. Such exchanges served as evidence of trust and goodwill and also provided hostages for the families involved. Some of these individuals may have chosen to remain with their adoptive peoples. This may account for some of the Algonkian women who were married to Huron men. On the other hand, Huron girls were never allowed to live with Algonkian families. Trading partnerships may also account for references to Huron men having kinsmen among the Neutral and Tionontati, with whom they sometimes left their children.

INTERNAL ECONOMY

The average Huron wished above all to be loved and respected by other members of his community and nation. His principal aim in acquiring wealth was to win affection and approval by sharing this wealth with others. Among the Huron, friendship was equated with, and maintained by, exchanges of gifts. Generosity was highly valued, and social status accrued to those individuals and groups who lavishly gave away their possessions. The acquisition of goods through hard work and trading with foreign groups was thus encouraged, although the possession of property was not valued as an end in itself.

This attitude toward property colored many aspects of Huron dealings with one another. The Huron did not have markets where they could gather to trade, and even individual barter was not a regular means for redistributing goods within the confederacy. Instead, economic activities were incorporated within a system of social relations in which hospitality, gift giving, and ceremonial exchanges played the major roles.

These attitudes encouraged a strong sense of communal responsibility. The Huron did not permit any member of a community to go without food and shelter. If a house and its contents were destroyed by fire, as happened frequently, the rest of the settlement helped its occupants to build a new one and presented them with corn, firewood, and household furnishings to make good their losses. On one occasion, all the households in Ossossané pledged to donate three vats of corn each and whatever else they could spare to help a number of orphans whose dwelling had been ravaged by fire. Visitors to a settlement were never refused food and lodging for as long as they wished to stay, although, if they could, they were expected to give their host a present as a formal expression of their friendship and thanks. Families vied with one another to provide feasts and entertainment for their neighbors, to contribute to the communal treasury when funds were needed for reparations payments, and to give presents when these were required for religious reasons. Such gifts were given willingly, since such generosity drew public acclaim and enhanced the donor's reputation. The raising of such funds was usually sponsored by the community council, and each present, along with its donor's name, was announced publicly. Presents were also publicly displayed at funerals and at curing ceremonies.

The strong disapproval people had of stinginess also created feelings of guilt which helped to encourage people to live up to Huron norms of generosity. A Huron who was particularly successful in hunting or trading feared that envious neighbors would seek to harm him or members of his family by means of witchcraft, and gift giving was believed to be the best way of averting this. It was also easy for the Huron to bring strong pressure to bear against anyone who refused to live up to their expectations of generosity. When Father Brébeuf was staying at the Attignawantan settlement of Toanché (*Teoenchen*), two fires ravaged the community, but spared the house of one of the settlement's largest and most prosperous families. This led to considerable resentment, and other villagers, either seriously or in jest, threatened to set fire to that house as well. To counteract this jealousy, the members of this household gave a feast to which the entire village was invited and turned over to their fellow villagers more than 120 measures of corn. Individuals who were consistently miserly and refused to participate in village activities were suspected of being witches, a serious crime since it exposed the accused to the danger of being slain.

Individual households produced most of the food and equipment that they needed. As a result, there were no strong economic ties holding Huron society together on a day-by-day basis. Individual households were capable of easily combining with or dissociating themselves from others. The unity of Huron society was largely based on shared ideals and mutual consent, not on economic necessity. Although some households were larger or more prosperous than others and their men were able to play leading roles in Huron public life, these differences were not sufficiently great to encourage the development of coercive forms of social control. Prestige was sought through public service and generosity, not through the hoarding of property, which its owners were unable to protect. The families of prominent chiefs, and members of their clan who lived in the same community, frequently found themselves working harder than anyone else to obtain the goods that had to be given away as presents to validate their collective status.

4/Warfare

Warfare was a pervasive fact of Huron life and influenced every aspect of the culture, no less than it did those of neighboring Iroquoian peoples. In their thinking, the Huron juxtaposed the forces and institutions of war and peace in a way that structured their behavior as markedly as did their dichotomy between forest and clearing. These two sets of concepts were in fact closely related. Life in the clearing and friendly trading relations with neighboring groups required men and women to exhibit moderation, generosity, and self-control and to forgive slights and injuries. The ideals of the warrior were the opposite of these: reckless bravery, self-assertiveness, and unquenchable anger directed against the enemies of the clearing. A warrior was expected to be fearless in confronting the enemy, unflinching when captured, and unyielding in his thirst for revenge. The Huron regarded these two sets of values as being antithetical, but equally necessary to maintain their existence. Their way of handling this dilemma was to separate the activities of peace and war. Each was the concern of different chiefs and councils, and sometimes disagreements between them over what policies should be followed were a source of tension in Huron life (Steckley 1978:80–81). While fighting was a man's business, women were caught up in warfare as victims, promoters demanding that the deaths of murdered kin be avenged, and participants in the torturing of enemy captives.

CAUSES OF WAR

It has often been claimed that warfare in early historic times was a struggle between the Iroquoian-speaking peoples and the Algonkians who lived east, west, and north of them. This idea evolved when it was believed that the Iroquoians had entered the Lower Great Lakes region only a few centuries before the Europeans. They were thus conceived of as a "disturbing cultural anomaly" that had forceably driven a wedge between the Algonkian peoples who were indigenous to the area. This had led the Algonkians to try to recover their lost lands and resulted in undying hostility between the two groups. The principal exception to this situation was the Huron, who curiously had chosen to trade rather than fight with the Algonkians.

A careful examination indicates that raiding was endemic among the horticultural peoples of the Lower Great Lakes region, whatever their linguistic affiliations. There is also no evidence that there was any more bitterness between the Iroquoians and Algonkians than there was between the various Iroquoian-speaking peoples. Peaceful relations were maintained only if there were compelling reasons to do so. The desire to obtain exotic goods was one reason to avoid war; the inability of a group to fight with all of its neighbors simultaneously was another. In both cases, political alliances were built around trading relations, although alliances concluded for economic reasons were far more likely to be enduring than were purely tactical ones. Prior to 1615 the Huron and Tionontati had been at war with one another, and, as late as 1624, a Huron war chief was trying to persuade his people to attack the Neutral. This suggests that until the development of the fur trade, the Huron were at least sporadically at war with the other Iroquoian peoples in Ontario. The peace that existed in historical times between the Neutral, on the one hand, and the Huron and Iroquois on the other, was probably the result of the landlocked Neutral trading for European goods with both of these confederacies, as well as of their need for peace with their eastern and northern neighbors in order to wage war more effectively against the Assistaronon who lived to the west of them.

While in the early seventeenth century the Huron were at war with all five of the Iroquois peoples, their principal adversaries were the Seneca, who lived nearest to them. According to the Huron, this war had been going on for over fifty years. There is no significant evidence in the archaeological record of warfare, or any other form of contact, between the Huron and the Iroquois prior to the sixteenth century. There is also no evidence that prior to when they obtained large quantities of guns from the Dutch in the 1640s, the Iroquois were more aggressive than the Huron or militarily superior to them. The struggle that was going on between these groups when they were first visited by the French appears to have been a more or less equal one, with neither side seeking to annihilate the other.

Another idea without foundation is that traditional Iroquoian warfare was a contest between neighboring groups for additional land or hunting territories. Even if early Iroquois attacks might have compelled some of the Huron peoples to move north and settle where they were living in the seventeenth century, their abandoned territory was not utilized by the Iroquois but remained part of the hunting grounds of the Huron confederacy. There is also no evidence of a shortage of arable land in Ontario or New York State. Through time, Iroquoian peoples tended to become concentrated in a smaller number of larger settlements, and, in south-central Ontario at least, many areas of good farmland that had been populated in earlier times were abandoned as more groups made their way north. There is no evidence of a lack of agricultural land, even in the historical Huron country, although eventually there might have been, had the occupation of the region continued for a long period.

Three principles motivated traditional warfare among all the Iroquoian-speaking peoples who inhabited the Lower Great Lakes region. First, it was the principal means by which young men acquired personal prestige and won a respected place for themselves as adult members of society. Every able-bodied man was expected to be a warrior, just as he was expected to be able to hunt, fish, and clear new fields. Boys were trained to use weapons from an early age and were encouraged to be brave, self-reliant, and uncomplaining. When warfare was not in progress, men sought opportunities to test their endurance and bravery. To become more nimble they cut incisions in the fat of their legs in order to harden them. They also held burning sticks against their arms until the flesh was scarred to see how long they could endure pain. A young man's greatest ambition was to demonstrate himself to be a successful warrior.

Second, warfare was the way in which injuries inflicted by members of one people or confederacy upon members of another were avenged. War was conceptualized as a prolonged blood feud in which each group killed members of the other in retaliation for previous killings. Since both the Huron and the Iroquois regarded such deaths as further injuries that had to be avenged, a state of continual conflict ensued. Families who had members slain in war or murdered by enemy raiders clamored for revenge and gave presents to the war chiefs to encourage them to attack the enemy. At the funerals of people who had been slain, their relatives demanded publicly that the wrong not go unpunished and that action be taken to ensure that the enemy was not tempted by any display of weakness to strike again. If men showed any slowness or reluctance to attack the enemy, the female relatives of the murdered person would accuse them of laziness or cowardice in order to force them to take to the field. Families of major chiefs, who could use their social influence to mobilize public support, were especially effective in fielding a large war party to avenge the murder of a kinsperson. There were occasional truces intended mainly to allow exchanges of prisoners. These were generally sought to secure the release of important chiefs.

Third, Iroquoian warfare was inspired by religious ideals. It was the means by which prisoners were obtained who were sacrificed by ritually torturing them to death. Among the Huron the spirit in whose honor this ritual was performed was Iouskeha, who also made the crops to grow and fish and game to thrive so that human beings had enough to eat. Iouskeha was identified with warfare, but also with the sun and all of the benevolent cosmic forces that made human life possible; hence prisoner sacrifice was interpreted as reinforcing and ensuring the continuation of the natural world upon which all life depended.

These three concepts were woven together in such a way that each one reinforced and complemented the other. The acts of daring that Huron warriors performed in enemy territory provided not only revenge for similar acts committed by the enemy against their own people but also a supply of captives for sacrifice. The method of sacrifice, in turn, provided the Huron with an opportunity to vent their hatred of the enemy on a particular victim, and gave the victim, as warrior, a final, spectacular opportunity to display his courage.

WAGING WAR

The Iroquoians did not wage war in the winter or in the spring and late fall when the leaves were off the trees and it was difficult to find cover. During the rest of the year, the Huron were on the alert for Iroquois raids, and rumors about enemy plans circulated from settlement to settlement. The larger Huron communities, especially on the southern and eastern perimeter of the country, were strongly palisaded and Huron chiefs endeavored to keep a sufficient number of men at home to protect their dwellings and the women working in the surrounding fields (they also used this as a method to limit the number of young men going to trade).

Huron chiefs sought to cultivate friends among neutral peoples, and better still among the enemy, who would give them advance warnings of attack. These might be resident foreigners, but even those Iroquois chiefs who hoped to make peace with the Huron so they could better fight some other group might secretly maintain contact with Huron chiefs and, as evidence of their goodwill, warn them of impending attacks through contacts in the Neutral country. Such men were given goodwill presents by Huron chiefs out of public funds, but were expected to vouch for the truth of any information they supplied by sending a gift of some value along with it.

The Huron who were engaged in warfare against the Iroquois dreaded similar informers in their midst and tried to identify them so that they could watch their activities and, if they were foreigners, kill or expel them before they became dangerous. Huron chiefs were very circumspect about their war plans and, while they allowed visitors to enter and leave the country, insisted that those they did not trust live in specially assigned houses and not travel about unattended. Huron chiefs who were friendly to the Iroquois could not be harmed or interfered with so long as they enjoyed the support and protection of their clan segment, but during episodes of major warfare they avoided antagonizing public feeling by expressing their opinions openly. They would once again have a public role to play when the Huron decided that peace with the Iroquois was necessary because they either had suffered a major defeat by the Iroquois or were anxious to recover someone who had been taken prisoner. Because of the factionalism and intergroup rivalries that prevailed in Iroquoian societies, opposing attitudes towards other groups were not uncommon. The Iroquoians seem to have regarded these as protecting them against total defeat, since they ensured that there were always chiefs who were in a favorable position to negotiate for peace with the enemy.

The kinds of campaigns that the Huron and Iroquois waged against each other varied from year to year. Sometimes a band of several hundred Huron warriors would lay siege to an Iroquois town. These men slowly made their way toward the Iroquois country, supporting themselves by hunting and fishing along the way. After they crossed Lake Ontario, they hid their canoes in the forest and moved on foot toward their objective, killing or taking prisoner any Iroquois they encountered. The siege of a community might last a week or more. Fires were set along the base of the palisade in order to challenge

Figure 12. Iroquois war camp under attack by Algonkians and their French allies, 1610. Huron camps would have been similar. From Champlain's Voyages *of 1613.*

the enemy to come out and fight. When they did, the opposing sides lined up and engaged in a pitched battle. After a few deaths or injuries on either side, the enemy retreated into their settlement, taking with them any prisoners they might have captured. The Huron usually built a temporary fort near the settlement, where they lived at night and could protect themselves against attack (Fig. 12), although they generally withdrew from the region before Iroquois reinforcements arrived from other settlements. To protect their withdrawal, the Huron stationed the old and wounded in the center and well-armed young warriors at the sides and rear. The seriously wounded were bound in a tightly flexed, often very painful, position and carried home in baskets on the backs of their companions. Occasionally, the Huron invited their Susquehannock allies to join them in attacking an Iroquois settlement.

If the Huron learned that a large Iroquois war party was approaching their country, warriors were sent out to ascertain the position of the enemy, while each of the major settlements strengthened its defenses until it was clear which one was going to be attacked. Meanwhile, the inhabitants of smaller communities prepared either to flee to the larger ones or to disperse in the forest. Depending on the number of the enemy, warriors came in from other communities to assist in defending the one that was threatened. These warriors helped to man the palisades and discouraged the enemy from attempting a surprise attack by making loud noises throughout the night.

Most years, between five hundred and six hundred young men set off for the Iroquois country. There, divided into groups of five or six men each, they hid in the fields or along paths in the forest hoping to capture a prisoner. At night more daring individuals would sneak into Iroquois settlements, where they entered houses and tried to hatchet one or more of the inhabitants. They would then attempt to set fire to the houses and escape in the resulting confusion. If possible, the prisoners were brought back to the Huron country alive; if not, they were clubbed to death, decapitated, and their scalps kept as trophies. Scalps (*onnonra*) were tanned and in time of war were fastened onto poles raised above the palisades of Huron settlements to intimidate attackers.

To prepare for these raids, a number of older and more daring war chiefs traveled from settlement to settlement, explaining their plans and distributing presents to gain support for their project. These chiefs had the right to determine where the warriors who joined their expedition would go and to dispose of the prisoners that were taken. The greatest enthusiasm for their plans was found among young men and families who wished to avenge members who had been slain by the Iroquois. To demonstrate prowess in fighting against the enemy was the most valued way for young men to acquire prestige, and this made each of them anxious to fight. Such prestige was especially desired because the important decisions affecting Huron life were made by older and more respected people. Young people, and especially young men, were regarded as unproved, and, therefore, as unreliable. The greatest opposition to war came from the older council chiefs, especially ones who were engaged in trade. They regularly expressed concern about the impact on Huron life of the reprisals that would follow. Many of these chiefs also feared that gaining prestige in war might give successful young warriors a greater say in village affairs, which could undermine their own authority and encourage the adoption of rash policies. Normally, the affairs of a community were publicly managed by the heads of clan groups and older men respected for their wisdom, but in times of crisis decision-making tended to pass into the hands of leading warriors.

Once support for an attack against the enemy had been gained at the village level, a general council was held at which, depending on the importance of the expedition, the decision was confirmed at the national or confederacy level. When the council was over, a war feast, which the women of families that supported the expedition had started to prepare before daybreak, was celebrated. At war feasts there was much singing and dancing. Led by the older war chiefs, the young warriors performed a dance in which, brandishing their weapons in mock combat, they made their way from one end of a longhouse to the other. To demonstrate that they did not lack courage, the recruits chanted curses and abuse against the enemy and promised themselves victory. Under the pretext of doing it in jest, warriors would knock down individuals whom they did not like. At the end of the feast, the various war parties left to invade enemy territory.

The origin of this war feast was attributed to a giant spirit whom a group of Huron had encountered while staying on the shore of a large lake. One of this group wounded the giant in the forehead because he failed to reply

Figure 13. A Huron warrior wearing slat armor. From Champlain's Voyages *of 1619.*

politely to their greeting. As a punishment, the giant sowed the seed of discord among human beings and, after revealing to them the war feast, another feast called the *onnonhwaroia*, and the war cry *wiiiiii*, he disappeared into the earth.

At the war feasts and while on the warpath, Huron warriors wore a circlet made of red moosehair around their heads. They also wore their finest necklaces and other ornaments. The reason that they gave for doing this was that, if pursued, they could throw these valuables behind them and escape while the enemy stopped to pick them up. These accoutrements also emphasized the ritual nature of war.

In war, as in hunting, the principal weapons were a wooden club and the bow and arrow. Before the introduction of iron arrowheads, warriors covered their back, legs, and other parts of their body with armor (*atientour*) made from thin strips of wood laced together with cords. This armor was proof against stone or bone-tipped arrows (Figs. 13, 14). They also had shields made of cedar bark, some of which covered the entire body (Steckley 1987b).

Each warrior carried with him a bag of roasted cornmeal that could be eaten without bothering to cook or even soak it in water. A bag would feed a man from six to eight weeks, after which the warriors returned home for a

Figure 14. Iroquoian warrior armed with a gun. From Novae Franciae Accurata Delineatio.

fresh supply, unless they were able to forage along the way. Bands carried with them a pennant, consisting of a piece of bark fastened to the end of a long stick. This was painted with the emblem of their community or nation. If the Huron found themselves trapped by the enemy, the older men would stay and fight while the younger ones tried to break out of their encirclement and escape into the forest.

Warriors sought supernatural support to assure success and avoid capture by the enemy. Particular attention was paid to dreams. If the patron spirit of warriors appeared as a dwarf and caressed the dreamer or struck him on the forehead, this foretold a successful campaign. Songs that would assure success were also revealed in dreams. If a man dreamed that he was captured by the enemy, he would sometimes insist that his friends torture him to prevent the dream from coming true. One man was tortured so severely as a result of his dream that he was unable to walk for six months.

Shamans were also consulted before setting out for war in an effort to foretell the future and avoid danger. One shaman sang inside a sweat lodge while the warriors danced outside. Finally his guardian spirit possessed him, and he said that he saw Iroquois raiders coming from the south and predicted that they would be put to flight and many taken prisoner. Cheered by this news, the war party set out to meet the foe. Other shamans claimed to be able to tell what was happening far off and were consulted by people whose relatives were at war. One old woman did this by tracing the outline of Lake Ontario in the sand and setting small fires on either side to represent the Huron warriors and their adversaries. From the behavior of these fires, she claimed to be able to tell what was happening to the warriors at that very moment.

TREATMENT OF PRISONERS

During their stay in the Iroquois country, Huron warriors sought to perform acts of daring that would win the respect of their companions and help them to acquire a good reputation back home. Nothing was as desirable, however, as to be credited with the capture of an enemy warrior. Women and children who were captured were usually tortured and killed on the spot. If they were taken back to the Huron country, it was to be adopted into Huron families to replace relatives who had been slain by the Iroquois. Able-bodied men were rarely slain at once, unless the Huron had captured too many of them or found that they endangered their security. From the moment of capture, men became the victims of a sadistic game in which the hope of escape or being returned to their people was balanced off against physical pain and the greater likelihood of an even more painful, but glorious, death. In their treatment of prisoners, the Huron revealed a dark side of the psychological finesse that was a prominent feature of their culture.

If the Huron came upon an enemy who was by himself, they surrounded him and said quietly "*sakien*" (sit down). His choice was to obey or be killed on the spot. In spite of the prospect of being tortured, most men preferred to surrender because they had hopes of escape or rescue at a later time.

As soon as the Huron had an enemy in their power, they tore out his fingernails and cut off the fingers that he used to draw a bow. This often caused a serious infection, but rarely resulted in the prisoner dying before he reached the Huron country. His neck and shoulders were cut with a knife and his arms bound with a special leather thong that warriors carried with them for this purpose. At the same time, the Huron made a speech to him about the cruelties that he and his people had practiced on them, saying that he now must be content to suffer likewise. Then they made him sing his war song. Each warrior had his own, which was revealed to him in a dream and which he sang to invoke supernatural help in time of danger. To show his courage, the prisoner often continued to sing all the way to the Huron country. Meanwhile, he was well fed so that he might better endure the tortures that awaited him.

A single warrior received the credit for each prisoner that was taken. If several warriors claimed the same prisoner, the prisoner had the right to designate his captor. He often named someone other than the man who was mainly responsible, hoping that this would arouse his real captor's jealousy and that the latter would secretly help him to escape rather than see the honor of his capture go to another. The possibility of getting his captors to fight among themselves was a source of hope for the prisoner.

While the capture of an enemy enhanced a warrior's reputation, it did not give him control over what happened to the prisoner. If men from more than one Huron people had participated in a war party, they held a council of war on the way home, in the course of which the prisoners were divided among them. Sometimes it was also decided to give a prisoner to the Hurons' Algonkian allies as a friendly gesture. When each group of warriors returned to their respective peoples, they turned their prisoners over to the war chiefs who had organized the raid, and these chiefs called national councils to decide which settlements and local clan groups should receive each prisoner. Feasts were also held to celebrate the victory. At these feasts, the warriors again performed their dances and chanted the praise of the "chiefs who had killed the enemy."

The prisoners were then led from one settlement to another until they reached the one to which they had been assigned. The treatment that they received at this time varied. A few, whose lives seemed likely to be spared either for permanent adoption or for prisoner exchanges, were dressed in fine beaver skins and treated with much kindness at each settlement. Sometimes dog feasts were given in their honor. Most, however, were stripped and bound hand and foot. They were painted and had strings or belts of wampum wound around their heads to indicate that they were victims destined to be tortured to death. As they approached each community, their captors led them slowly between two lines of its inhabitants, who tortured them with clubs, thorns, knives, and firebrands. Everywhere they were taken, the prisoners were expected to sing.

Each prisoner was formally adopted by a family that had a member killed by the Iroquois. The prisoner symbolically replaced the lost relative and served to dry the tears of the bereaved. This equation of enemies and kinspeople probably was reinforced by the belief that because the Iroquois had eaten Huron prisoners they had acquired something of a Huron nature. Normally, prisoners, who were a scarce commodity, were made available only to the most prominent families in reciprocation for their own exceptional generosity to other Huron. In one case, a prisoner was turned over to an important chief of the northern Attignawantan community of Arontaen to replace a nephew who had been captured by the Iroquois.

Adoption was an important step in determining a prisoner's fate. If for some reason, his appearance, manners, or skills pleased his adoptive family, they might decide to spare his life, and he would assume the name and titles of the dead Huron he replaced. As with the Iroquois women and children who were brought to the Huron country, efforts would be made to turn him gradually into a loyal member of his new family. In time he might even accompany the Huron to war against his own people. Exploiting the prisoner's insecurity played a crucial role in this transformation. For a number of years after his adoptive family decided not to torture him, there was the danger that if he displeased them in any way, they might decide to kill him. During this period, bouts of hard labor and abuse would alternate with extended periods when he was treated as if he really were a Huron. Thus he was subjected to great pressure to identify with his role as a member of the family as the one offering him the best chance of survival. Any prisoner who tried to escape and failed would be killed.

Such adoptions were, however, quite rare for adult male prisoners. More often their "caressing" was by torture. The village as a whole looked forward to such an event, and the battered condition of many prisoners allowed their adoptive relatives to explain to them that ordering their death was an act of kindness befitting a conscientious parent.

Even after a prisoner's adoptive relatives had condemned him to die, they continued to treat him with courtesy and an outward show of affection, as if he truly were their murdered kinsman. Although he was tied so he could not escape, the women of the family wept when they fed him, and the men would give him their pipes to smoke, wipe the sweat from his face, and fan him if he were hot. By using the prisoner to recall their dead relative in as vivid a manner as possible, the family was able to work up greater enthusiasm to avenge his murder.

Very often the chiefs and old men of the community who were guarding the prisoner would talk to him about his capture and question him closely about what was happening among his people. This was done quietly, and no attempt was made to extract any information by torture. Before he was slain, the prisoner was provided with the means to celebrate an *atsataion*, or farewell feast, such as was given by Huron who believed themselves about to die. Everyone was invited to attend the feast, the food being provided by the prisoner's newfound relatives and executioners. Before the meal began, he walked through the longhouse and in a courteous manner inviting the Huron to amuse themselves killing him, assuring them that he did not fear death. Then he sang and danced the length of the house, with the Huron joining in. It was extremely important for a prisoner to behave bravely at this time and throughout the gruesome torture that followed. Such behavior not only demonstrated his courage; it spelled misfortune for his tormentors if they could not compel him to cry out and plead for mercy. Thus the prisoner could still engage in symbolic warfare with the enemy even as they were killing him.

The torturing of a prisoner might last only for a single night or for as long as five or six days. The entire community and people from surrounding settlements assembled to watch and participate in the event. On the first evening they gathered in the house of the principal war chief of the town, the older people mounting the sleeping platforms that ran along either side of the house, the younger and more active ones filling the central aisle below. Before the prisoner was brought in, the chief reminded those who had assembled that torturing a prisoner was an important act that was witnessed by Iouskeha, the patron spirit of warriors. The chief also warned those present to be careful to burn only the prisoner's legs at the beginning so that he would not die before dawn. The concern that the prisoner should not die before sunrise was indicative of the sacred aspect of the torture that was to follow, the sun being a manifestation of Iouskeha. The sacred nature of the event was further emphasized by the chief's order that everyone should refrain from sexual intercourse that night and behave in an orderly and restrained fashion. Avoidance of sexual intercourse was a method of concentrating supernatural power that was associated with the performance of many religious rituals.

At this point the prisoner was led in. He was stripped of whatever clothes he still wore and his hands were bound together. It was announced to what chiefs the main parts of his body would be given after he had been killed, the head, arms, and liver being regarded as choice portions. The prisoner was then forced to make his way back and forth from one end of the longhouse to the other, while all who were within reach armed themselves with a brand or a burning piece of bark, which they thrust at him as he passed. To increase his torment the Huron also tried to force him to run through the hearths that were blazing down the center of the longhouse. At the ends of the aisle he was frequently stopped and made to rest on hot ashes taken from the fire. There the bones of his hands were broken, his ears pierced with burning sticks, and his wrists burned or cut through by wrapping cords around them and pulling them back and forth as fast as possible. Later, fire was applied to his genitals. Sometimes, while a prisoner was making his way from one end of the longhouse to the other, he was able to scatter clouds of dust and ashes from the fireplaces or even to set the house on fire. He hoped to make his escape in the resulting confusion. While it is unlikely that any prisoner had much of a chance of escaping from the settlement, and even less of being able to make his way home, the thought that this was possible continued to sustain him, although to an ever lesser extent as his wounds increased. Eventually his strength began to fail him, so that he had to be carried through the longhouse. At this point, the chiefs ordered the people to stop torturing him so that he would live until sunrise. The prisoner was then laid on a mat and allowed to rest, while many people left for a breath of fresh air.

When he began to revive, he was forced to sing once more and his torture began anew. Prior to this time, the principal attacks had been aimed at the extremities of his body. These were designed to make him suffer, but were not meant to endanger his life immediately. Now, when the prisoner was no longer able to move about easily, torture was applied to his entire body, mainly by the youths of the village. They made cuts in his arms, legs, thighs, and other fleshy parts, quenching the flow of blood by thrusting glowing brands into the wounds. His tormentors patiently waited their turn and showed no signs of anger or lack of self-control. Their speeches sounded like those of friends. One youth would say that he was caulking a canoe for the prisoner, at the same time burning his body in imitation of the process; another would express regret that the prisoner was cold and proceed to warm him by roasting his flesh; still a third would protest that he knew nothing about torture, while cutting out the prisoner's gonads. During this phase of the torture, every part of the prisoner's body was cut, burned, or bruised. From time to time, the

Figure 15. Torture of a war captive. From Novae Franciae Accurata Delineatio.

Huron gave him something to eat or poured a little water into his mouth so that he would last through the night. The Huron also redoubled their efforts to make the prisoner cry out as much as possible. Occasionally, their mock benevolence wore thin and they taunted him, saying that he and his people had killed Huron thinking that retribution would never be forthcoming, and he must now suffer a deserved fate.

On the morning the prisoner was to die, fires were lighted before dawn around a scaffold two meters high that had been erected outside the settlement. The prisoner was led to the scaffold and tied, either facing an upright pole (Fig.15) or to the branch of a tree that passed overhead. In either case, this was done in such a way that he was free to move. The Huron enjoyed watching a prisoner play up to torture and at no time bound him so tightly that he was immobilized. Once he was securely fastened, they continued to burn his body, but also began to attack his vital organs. Brands were thrust down his throat and into his eyes and rectum and he was made to eat pieces of his own flesh. During this period he was prevented from sitting down by brands thrust through the platform from below, which also burned his feet. Later he was scalped and burning pine gum was poured over his head. When it was clear that he was about to die, his head was either cut off or broken open with a club. At the same time, the Huron cut out his heart and chopped off his hands and feet. Then they cut open his belly and gave all the children small pieces of his bowels, which they hung on the ends of sticks and carried through the settlement as symbols of victory.

If the prisoner had been particularly brave, the Huron would roast his heart, which was the organ they believed was associated with courage. Bits of it were then eaten by the young men in an effort to ingest his bravery. Some men also made cuts in their neck and let his blood run into their arteries, because they believed this would prevent them from ever being surprised by the enemy. The prisoner's body was then cut up in order to be cooked and eaten. Some ate his flesh with horror; others relished it. All of them regarded this as an act that was primarily of religious significance.

After sunset on the day the prisoner was killed, everyone made loud noises to drive his soul from the settlement. The souls of warriors who had died bravely were considered dangerous and the Huron did not want them to linger around their homes. Instead of being honored, the cooked bones of prisoners were discarded in the middens like any other form of garbage.

THE MEANING OF WARFARE

John Witthoft (1959) has argued that as corn horticulture replaced hunting as the dominant mode of subsistence, the resulting decline in the role of men as food producers led them to seek more prestige as warriors. At the same time, women projected their resentment at the lack of male participation in routine tasks by transforming their traditional role as butchers of game into a new one as butchers of male captives. This theory has two main weaknesses. First, it ignores the importance of hunting and fishing for Iroquoian subsistence and also the routine work performed by men in clearing new fields, a task that was as arduous as planting and tending the crops. Second, men as well as women played an active role in torturing prisoners.

In spite of these qualifications, there are some valid points in Witthoft's analysis. In early times, hunting, especially as it was carried out during the winter, probably provided the principal measure of an individual man's courage and his ability to use weapons. Fishing and clearing fields required energy and devotion, but such activities do not appear to have provided Iroquoian men with an opportunity to acquire an appreciable amount of prestige in relation to one another. Even hunting had become largely a team effort. Thus its lessening importance may have been an important factor promoting a growing interest in warfare. Even if the growth of confederacies served to suppress local warfare, the conflicts that continued between confederacies indicate that by the historical period warfare was essential to the social organization of all the northern Iroquoian peoples. This was probably true because it was the principal means by which young men could acquire individual prestige and win for themselves an enduring reputation that would allow them to play a significant role in the social and political life of their communities.

The severity with which prisoners were tortured may have been partly a projection of hostilities that were generated by the need to repress the expression of resentment, jealousy, and anger within Huron society. It also may have been encouraged by the tensions that were produced by the constant threat of death that all Iroquoian peoples faced as a result of endemic warfare. Yet, while the search for revenge and individual prestige appear to be indigenous aspects of warfare in the Lower Great Lakes region, the sacrificial cult contained numerous elements that, like corn horticulture, were derived from the southeastern United States, and ultimately from Mesoamerica (Knowles 1940; Rands and Riley 1958). These traits included the sacrifice of prisoners, the removal of the heart, the killing of the victim on an elevated platform and in view of the sun, and the cooking and eating of all or part of the body. While there are significant differences between the sacrificial cult as it was practiced in the southeastern United States and among the northern Iroquoians, these differences merely indicate that it did not diffuse in its entirety from one region to another. Instead, certain key ideas seem to have spread north and were used by the Iroquoians to develop a sacrificial complex of their own.

The basic concept linking Iroquoian beliefs about death through warfare and prisoner sacrifice with those found in Mesoamerica was a common religious conviction that only through the sacrifice of human blood could the cosmic order be maintained. Just as nature, by sacrificing the lives of plants and animals, provided the energy that sustained human existence, so human beings had to help sustain the powers of the cosmos through the reciprocal sacrifice of their own vital forces. Yet the relationship of men and women to the cosmic cycle was totally different. Huron women sustained human existence, in a creative and nurturing fashion, by growing crops, giving birth to children, and caring for their families. In their everyday life, men appropriated energy from the natural world by means of violence and destruction: cutting down forests and killing fish and game animals. Within the human realm, they sustained society by waging war to protect their communities and avenge murdered kinspeople. Yet, through the sacrifice of their own blood to sustain the sun, men also helped to maintain the cosmic order upon which all living things depended. Hence, among the Huron and all the other northern Iroquoian peoples, prisoner sacrifice was the means by which men, by performing violent acts, could claim a positive and nurturing role for themselves in the maintenance of the cosmic order upon which everything depended.

5/Kinship and Family Life

If a gender-based division of labor and the distinction between forest and clearing constituted the basic structures of Huron subsistence activities, kinship relations grounded in the nuclear family provided the core from which, by real or metaphorical extension, most of the key features of Huron social and political organization were created.

PEOPLES AND CLANS

Every Huron simultaneously belonged to one of four peoples or nations (tribes) and one of eight clans. Each people was made up of one or more communities located close to each other in a specific territory. The largest of the Huron peoples was the Attignawantan, which consisted of over a dozen communities, while the smallest was the Tahontaenrat, which inhabited only one large town. While at least some of these peoples claimed great antiquity, it is clear that each of them had grown over time through the incorporation of extended families, communities, and smaller peoples. During the sixteenth century, amalgamation of this sort dramatically reduced the number of separate "nations," as smaller and geographically dispersed groups joined together to form the four Huron peoples. If groups that called themselves the Attignawantan and Attigneenongnahac existed as early as 1450, as they claim to have done, they were no doubt very different, and smaller, groups at that time than they were in the seventeenth century. Other peoples may have acquired their historical identity at a much later date. As we have already seen, the largest of the Huron peoples, the Attignawantan, was very weakly unified and often threatened by regional divisions. The Huron do not appear to have regarded their "nations" as other than political groupings of people who were prepared to live close to one another and defend a common territory.

At the same time, every Huron belonged to one of eight clans (*yentiokwa*), which were named after various animals: Bear, Deer, Turtle, Beaver, Wolf, Sturgeon (or Loon), Hawk, and Fox (Steckley 1982a). Clans were conceptualized as kinship groupings, the people belonging to groups sharing the same name claiming descent from a common ancestor. There is, however, no evidence that everyone who belonged to a particular clan was biologically or genealogically related. Clanship had no territorial implications, and members of the same clan were found living in many communities and throughout the whole Huron country. Even Huron, Neutral, and Iroquois who belonged to clans named after the same animal regarded themselves as bound by many of the same ties of affinity as were members of a single clan within their home community (Tooker 1970). Membership in the same clan was used to facilitate social and political interaction between different communities and different peoples. Upon arriving in a community, a stranger would first seek out members of the same clan that he belonged to, as it was from them that he would expect protection and hospitality. This was even true of Huron and Iroquois chiefs visiting each other's country to discuss occasional truces.

An individual was a member of the same clan to which his or her mother belonged. Marriage between people who belonged to the same clan, even if they were members of different peoples or confederacies, was regarded as a form of incest. Hence a Huron's father and mother belonged to different clans and marriage was a means of linking clans together. It did this most effectively within the community and the nation, where intermarrying occurred most commonly.

The clan played its primary political role at the community level. Members of a community who belonged to the same clan constituted a well-defined grouping of considerable social and political importance. For convenience, we may term these local groupings clan segments. Each clan segment, which normally had from 250–300 members, was made up of several matrilineages whose members occupied about ten matrilineally constituted extended families (*ahwatsira*). While the members of households that belonged to the same matrilineage were genealogically closely related, it is not known whether the members of clan segments could accurately trace their descent from a known female ancestor or if their kin ties were partly fictional. The Hurons' lack of interest in genealogies, and the occasional movement of a nuclear family from one longhouse to another (not necessarily in the same clan segment) suggest the latter. Every clan segment had its own chiefs, who managed its affairs and represented it on the community, national, and confederacy councils. Because these offices were clan privileges, a chief could never transmit his position to his son, since his son was not a member of his clan. Instead, his office passed to a brother or to one of his sister's sons. The clan segment was the primary unit responsible for protecting its members from harm and for securing reparations for injuries done to them either by members of that clan segment or by outsiders.

Some small villages may have been composed of a nucleus of women and children who belonged to the same clan segment. Larger settlements, however, were composed of as many as six or seven clan segments. In the latter settlements, each clan segment occupied a separate section of the community. Individual segments remained sufficiently independent of one another to be able to leave a community and either join another or found one of their own if they felt they were not being fairly treated. When towns such as Khinonascarant and Cahiagué split apart to form two or more new ones, the cleavages were normally between clan segments or groups of clan segments. Likewise, there are examples of two or more small villages, each containing only one clan segment, joining together to form a large multisegmented community. These changes were most likely to occur when settlements were moving from one clearing to another as part of their pattern of long term relocation.

The individual Huron household rarely consisted of a nuclear family; instead five or six nuclear families, each composed of a husband, wife, their children, and occasionally another relative, lived together in the same longhouse. A normal household consisted of a mother and her grown daughters, or a group of sisters, living together with their husbands and children. Married men went to live with their wives' families. Brébeuf observed that a woman exercised lifelong jural authority over her daughters. In the Huron context, this meant that a woman recognized her mother or grandmother as the head of her household and normally deferred to her wishes. Throughout his adult life, every Huron man had obligations to assist both his mother's household and that of his wife. This included provisioning them with fish, meat, and furs. The older women in each longhouse tended to be highly critical of men who had married into their extended family if they failed to work hard in order to live up to their obligations. If a man was especially lazy or neglectful, they might even pressure his wife to divorce him. Once she agreed, no more was required than to gather up his possessions and drop them outside the door of the house. Such a man had no choice but to return to the longhouse of his mother and sisters. If they too were annoyed with him, his mother or sisters might, for a time, refuse to let him live with them, making him an object of public ridicule.

Archaeological and physical anthropological evidence indicates that prior to the development of a horticultural economy, the Iroquoian-speaking peoples of Ontario had a patrilocal band structure: a father and his sons would normally remain together throughout their lives, while, upon marriage, women would move from one band to another (Spence 1986). This arrangement was a very efficient one in a society that depended largely upon hunting, and hence particularly upon male cooperation, for its survival. The Iroquoian matrilocal residence pattern seems to have evolved after a new division of labor resulted in men being away from their communities, performing a variety of different tasks in small scattered groups, for much of the year, while women remained in their home communities in daily face-to-face contact. Under these circumstances, it became desirable for several generations of related women to live together and help each other and for men, when they were home, to live with their wives' families. The development of corn horticulture and matrilineal residence also allowed larger extended families to develop, not only because the new subsistence pattern made it possible to feed larger numbers, but also because closely related women generally find it easier to live together than do unrelated women (Ember 1973). Matrilocal residence also encouraged the development of matrilocal descent groups and the matrilineal inheritance of clan membership and clan offices.

Not all Huron households corresponded with this matrilocal pattern. In some of them, women were living with their husband's relatives (Richards 1967). There is also evidence of married women living in settlements other than the one in which they were born. The majority of these households appear to have been those of chiefs. In these cases it may be that, in order to ensure that a chief would continue to live with his clan segment, one or more prospective heirs to such an office went to live with their mother's brother. In this way an extended household, although matrilineal, would be made up at least partly of a man and his nephews rather than a woman and her daughters. There is, however, no clear evidence that this practice was known among the Huron. Other variations from a matrilocal norm may have been caused by idiosyncratic factors, such as the amount of space that was available and the rank and personal preferences of the married couple.

Clans played a significant role in Huron political and ritual life. Among their other duties, they were responsible for helping to settle blood feuds. When the Jesuits were given reparations payments for the murder of a young French assistant in 1648, these were made by chiefs representing the "eight nations" of the Huron. In this context, "nation" was the French translation of the Huron word for clan. Clans were especially effective in settling disputes between communities or political divisions because they cut across Huron political organization and the same ones were found among all four Huron peoples.

For various ritual purposes, the eight Huron clans were grouped to form three phratries, or assemblages of clans, called Bear, Turtle, and Wolf. The Bear phratry contained the Bear and Deer clans; the Turtle phratry the Turtle and Beaver clans; and the Wolf phratry the Wolf, Hawk, Sturgeon, and Fox clans. When only two divisions were required, as, for example, for the burial of the dead and the condolence of their families, the Bear and Turtle phratries were combined to form a single Bear/Turtle moiety opposing the Wolf moiety. John Steckley (1982a) has suggested that in the original constitution of the Huron confederacy, the Attignawantan people may have been ritually identified with the Bear/Turtle moiety and the Attigneenongnahac with the Wolf moiety. Later the Attignawantan sat on one side of the fire at meetings of the confederacy, while the three remaining tribes sat on the other. It is possible that the northern Attignawantan, whose leader, Aennons, was a member of the Bear clan, was ritually identified with the Bear clan, while the southern Attignawantan was identified with the Turtle clan. This may indicate that the rivalry between these two Attignawantan groups was a longstanding one embedded in ritual as well as political considerations. It also suggests that clan and moiety organization may have given meaning to divisive as well as integrative behavior in Huron society.

KINSHIP

In his dictionary, Sagard listed, without further explanation, the following Huron kin terms: father, *aystan* or *aihtaha*; mother, *anan* or *ondoüen*; son or daughter, *ayein*; brother or sister, *ataquen*; younger brother, *ohienha*; grandfather, *ochata*; uncle, *hoüatinoron*; aunt, *harha*; nephew or niece, *hi-uoitan*; niece ("manière de parler aux femmes"), *etchondray*; cousin, *earassé*; father-in-law, *yaguenesse*; son-in-law, *agueinhesse*; brother-in-law, *eyakin*; sister-in-law, *nidaunoy*. Apparently he did not detect the subtle differences in their terms for son and daughter, brother and sister. The kinship terms that Sagard noted are for the most part very similar to Wyandot ones that were systematically recorded in the nineteenth century (Morgan 1871) and that provide the most complete evidence of how the Huron kinship system worked. Like other Iroquoian systems, Wyandot extended the term for mother (*ahnǎ'uh*) to include mother's sister and also used the term for father (*hiese'tǎ*) for father's brother. They had special terms for both mother's brother (*hä-wäteno'rä*) and father's sister (*ahrä'hoc*). Parallel cousins (father's brothers' and mother's sisters' children) were called brother and sister; the word *cousin* (*järä'seh*) being reserved for cross-cousins (father's sisters' and mother's brothers' children). A man referred to the children of his sister, female parallel cousins, and female cross-cousins as his nieces (*yashonedrä'ka*) and nephews (*hashonedrä'ka*); the children of his brother, male parallel cousins, and male cross-cousins were called his sons (*aneah'*) and daughters (*eneah'*). In the case of women the situation was reversed; children of sisters and other female consanguineal (blood) relatives of the same generation were called sons and daughters, while the children of male consanguineal relatives of that generation were called nieces (*ewäteh*) and nephews (*hewäteh*). All consanguineal relatives of the second ascending generation were called grandfather (*hä-shutä'*) and grandmother (*ahshutä'*) and those of the second descending generation were called grandson (*hatra'ah*) and granddaughter (*yatra'ah*). There were separate terms for older and younger brother (*haye'uh/hayea'hä*) and older and younger sister (*aye'uh/yayeah'hä*). A situation apparently unique among the northern Iroquoians was the Wyandots' use of the term "father's sister" (*ahrä'hoc*) to refer to mother's brother's wife and their reciprocal use of "mother's brother" (*häwäteno'rä*) for father's sister's husband.

The matrilineal principles that governed residence, clan membership, and the inheritance of offices are not strongly reflected in Wyandot or other northern Iroquoian kinship terminology. In a person's parental generation, kinspeople of the same sex who were members of the same clan were terminologically distinguished from members of other clans. In a speaker's own generation, however, cross-cousins and parallel cousins were distinguished from one another, with no attention being paid to whether they were on the father's or mother's side. In the next generation, the distinction between who were called sons and daughters depended on whether their parents were of the same or opposite sex from the speaker. The sex of the speaker also determined the terms that were used for nieces and nephews, and there is evidence that a century earlier the Wyandot had distinguished between maternally and paternally linked grandparents and grandchildren (Poitier 1920:108). Sex linkages counted for a great deal in this system, while lineage and clan membership counted for much less. This suggests that kinship terminology reflected a bilateral rather than a unilineal social organization. While the matrilineal extended family was the building block of clan segments, and, metaphorically, of moieties and ultimately the Huron confederacy, individual Huron maintained numerous connections with their father's as well as their mother's family. While their primary orientation was to their matrilineal extended family, relatives, especially male ones, on the father's side might be called on for help in mutual aid activities, such as forest clearance, house building, and avenging a murder.

HOUSES

The typical Huron longhouse (*yannonchia*) was a windowless structure about 6.5 meters wide and approximately the same height. Archaeological evidence indicates that a few houses were over forty-six meters long but that they averaged only eighteen meters. It also reveals that the average house had three hearths (Dodd 1984). This confirms the Jesuit census, which indicates that the average Huron and Tionontati longhouse contained 2.86 hearths. Since each hearth was normally used by two families, this suggests that six families, and possibly thirty to thirty-six people, lived in an average longhouse. Conditions within the longhouse were quite cramped, with only 2.5–3.5 square meters of floor space per person. In prehistoric times, the average length of longhouses was considerably greater than in the historical period. While it is not certain that the number of families that inhabited a longhouse was directly proportional to its length (living conditions may have been more cramped in the larger settlements of the historical period), this suggests that the average size of an extended family had declined, perhaps because by the historical period many of the functions of looking after collective welfare that had once been carried out by the extended family were now attended to by the clan segment. Smaller extended families also lessened the loss resulting from any one longhouse catching on fire.

Despite what must have been their shaggy and often dilapidated appearance, Huron longhouses were a marvel of construction. They consisted of a wooden frame covered with slabs of bark; the whole of this had to be strong enough to withstand gale-force winds and heavy snowfalls. The walls of the house consisted of vertical support poles, sharpened at the bottom and twisted or pushed sixty to eighty centimeters into the ground. These poles were usually of eastern white cedar, which had an average use-life in the ground of over twenty-six years, far longer than that of poles made of any other wood (Warrick 1988). The vertical support poles were reinforced with horizontal ones that were lashed to them with shredded bark or rope. Both the vertical and horizontal supports were seven to nine centimeters in diameter. The roof consisted of additional poles, which were fastened to the uprights and then bent together and tied in the center to form a semicircular arch (Fig. 16). The entire framework was covered with slabs of bark that, when necessary, had been softened in steam or hot water to make them more pliable. Cedar

Figure 16. Iroquoian longhouse, based on John Bartram's diagram of an Onondaga longhouse of 1743. Huron ones would have been similar, although most were tapered at each end.

bark was considered to be the best covering, although it was extremely flammable and resulted in conflagrations that destroyed entire communities. Elm bark, which was also used as a covering, was scarcely less dangerous. The slabs of bark were tied to the wooden frame and held down by a network of saplings (Steckley 1987a). Most Huron houses had tapered or rounded, and only very rarely rectangular, ends. Doors were located at the ends, and sometimes along the sides of the longhouses. Holes were left in the roof to permit smoke to escape and let in a little light. These smokeholes could be closed in bad weather. If more room was needed, the length of the house was increased by removing one end and adding a new section. Because Huron communities did not remain in one place for more than a few decades, houses were not built to last for a long time. In their selection of materials and construction techniques, the Huron sought to construct with minimum effort a dwelling that would serve their needs.

The Huron frequently aligned their houses so that one end was facing northwestward into the prevailing winter winds (Norcliffe and Heidenreich 1974). This may have been done to reduce the chances of houses being blown down by strong winds coming off Georgian Bay. It also lessened the danger of fire spreading from one house to another, since the prevailing wind would drive the flames along a single dwelling rather than towards others. The length of each house made it necessary to align a number of them side by side in order to conserve space. These groupings of houses may to some degree reflect the clan structure of the community. Houses were ideally kept three or four paces apart in order to minimize the danger of fire spreading from one to another. They were also ideally set back from the palisade that surrounded the community in order to make it easier for warriors to defend the settlement. In actual fact, both rules were frequently violated as the Huron attempted to pack as many houses as possible into a confined space. Some of the larger settlements had open spaces between the ends of houses. These were used to dispose of garbage rather than for public activities. Most of the important Huron celebrations took place either indoors or in the clearings outside of the settlements.

In each settlement at least one house was deliberately made larger than the rest. This house belonged to a leading chief and was the main place where feasts and meetings were held. In some villages there were two such houses. One belonged to the leading civil chief, the other to the leading war chief. The house of Atsen, the war chief who lived in the Attignawantan community of Arontaen, was called *otinnontsiskiaj ondaon*, "the house of cut-off heads." It was the place where the main councils of war were held and where prisoners who were brought to the community were tortured. Domestic affairs were discussed in the *endionhra ondaon*, "the house of council." In the largest settlements, each clan segment had one or two meeting houses, while the residence of the principal chief served as the meeting place for the whole community.

The exteriors of Huron houses were decorated with paintings, mostly done in red ochre. Some indicated the clan or lineage affiliations of their inhabitants; others were done purely for pleasure. At one or both ends of the longhouse was an enclosed porch, where firewood, corn, preserved fish, and other goods were stored. The corn and fish were kept in large bark vats. Along the interior central aisle two strong poles ran the length of the house. These were used for suspending cooking pots and also as racks from which clothing and provisions could be hung to keep them dry. Beneath these racks was a row of large fireplaces, each about three meters apart. These were kept burning all the time for cooking, to provide light in these windowless structures, and to keep people warm in the cold weather. Sheets of bark covered the ground along both sides of the longhouse and over this, running the length of the longhouse, there was normally a bark platform, solidly supported and raised up to 1.5 meters off the ground. In the winter, when the Huron slept on the lower level near the fires, these platforms served as a canopy. In the summer, if people did not sleep in the open air, they slept on top of these platforms to escape the fleas. There were bark partitions between the fireplaces, but not between the families that lived on either side of a fireplace. Hence, there were few opportunities for any family to enjoy much privacy.

Although the Huron lived in crowded conditions, their behavior in their homes and settlements was noted for its cooperativeness and tranquility. Brébeuf commented at length on the love and unity that existed among them and on their kindness towards each other as they coped with famine, sickness, and death. The Huron were also noted for their generosity. Any stranger to a community, unless he came from a hostile people, was immediately made welcome. When he arrived at a house, his host lighted a pipe and, after smoking it himself, passed it to him as a sign of welcome. If food was being served, it was offered to the guest. No invitation was required to stay with any household, and a guest was normally welcome to remain as long as he wanted. A concern not to offend other people made the Huron punctilious in visiting one another and attending feasts and dances. They were not easily annoyed and concealed wrongs done to them rather than make a public show of anger. Living in communal houses and in crowded villages, the Huron strove to keep disruptive behavior to a minimum and to externalize their aggression along carefully controlled lines.

Although Huron women regularly swept their houses, life in them was made troublesome by smoke, dogs, and vermin and by young children urinating on the floors. In spite of the care that women took to gather wood that was dry and smoke-free, not all of the smoke from their fireplaces escaped through the holes in the roof. Attempts to work with defective lighting inside the houses during the wintertime must have produced eyestrain. When more light was needed to work by, small torches were made out of conical rolls of birch bark, and these gave off still more smoke. Because of this smoke, eye diseases were common, and many older people became blind. Large numbers of dogs roamed about freely inside the houses. They often knocked over and broke cooking pots and helped themselves to food whenever they wished. Mice and fleas were common in the houses, the latter no doubt because of the dogs. Women periodically tried to drive the lice from their furs and from their bodies and those of their children. As they caught the lice they ate them, saying this was in retaliation for the suffering they inflicted upon humans.

Huron houses were sparsely furnished. Moveable sheets of bark covered the doorways, and in the winter a large hide or blanket was added as extra protection against the snow and cold. Mats were used to sit and sleep on. Every Huron had his or her own mat and, when it was spread out, it served to designate each person's place in the longhouse. During the winter, the Huron covered themselves with hides at night; in warmer weather they slept in whatever clothes they were wearing. The benches running along either side of the house served as places to sit. Most work was done kneeling or squatting either on these platforms or on the floor. Because of the danger of fire, the Huron placed their most valuable possessions in boxes and buried them in shallow pits, both inside and outside their houses. Some seed corn may also have been stored underground to protect it against fire.

COOKING

Cooking was a woman's job. Except occasionally in summer, when meals may have been prepared out of doors, it was done at the family fireplace inside the longhouse. While these hearths were generally kept burning all the time, if fire had to be made it was done by rubbing one stick inside the hollow of another. Although the Huron lived in extended families, regular meals were cooked and eaten separately by each nuclear family. The Huron normally consumed two meals a day, one in the morning, the other in the evening, although they ate informally whenever they felt hungry and food was at hand throughout the day. They did not wash their hands before eating, but, if they were greasy, they might wipe them on their hair or the fur of a nearby dog.

Figure 17. Huron woman grinding corn. From Champlain's Voyages *of 1619.*

They also did not clean their cooking and eating utensils very often, although each person appears to have had his or her own spoon and bowl. They also belched without inhibition during their meals.

Corn was the single most important item in their diet. After the kernels had thoroughly dried, women removed them from the cobs and stored them until they needed them for food. Then they either pounded them into flour in a mortar hollowed out of a tree trunk using a pole about two meters long (Fig. 17) or else ground them between two stones. The best and most grit-free flour was produced using the wooden mortar. The husks were removed with bark fans.

Although the Huron prepared many different dishes, most of their cuisine consisted of variations on a few basic themes. Their most common food was a thin soup made of cornmeal boiled in water. This eliminated the need to prepare drinks separately. It was varied by adding slices of fish, meat, or squash. Fish, either whole or eviscerated, were dropped into the pot and after being boiled for a time were removed, pounded into a mash, and then returned to it. No attempt was made at this time to remove the bones, scales, and entrails. At special feasts a thick corn soup was prepared and served with fat or oil poured over it. Soup was also made from roasted kernels of corn mixed with beans, and from *andohi*. The latter were immature ears of corn that had been allowed to ferment for several months in a pool of stagnant water. *Andohi* was regarded as a special delicacy.

The Huron also ate unleavened bread, which they cooked under the ashes. To give it more flavor, dried fruit and small bits of deer fat were sometimes mixed into the dough, which was fashioned into cakes a few centimeters long. These cakes were either wrapped in fresh corn leaves or stuck directly into the ashes. When the latter procedure was followed, the bread was washed before it was eaten. In the summer, special bread was made from fresh corn, which the women masticated and then pounded in a large mortar. The soft paste that was produced in this fashion was wrapped in corn leaves and baked. Huron women also baked ears of corn and slices of squash, as well as *andohi*. They roasted fish and meat. In the summer, everyone enjoyed sucking the juice from ripe cornstalks. They did not use salt, but occasionally threw a handful of ashes into their soup, which, in addition to improving its flavor, supplied minerals to their diet.

CHILDHOOD

Children were highly valued in Huron society. Births were widely spaced, and many children did not live to adulthood. Few families had more than three living children. A family celebrated the birth of a girl more than it did that of a boy. This reflected the matrilineal basis of the extended family, as well as the special value that the Huron placed on woman as childbearers. Despite their small nuclear families and matrilineal bias, the Huron hoped to have numerous descendants of both sexes to care for them in their old age and protect them from their enemies. It was a reproach to say to a Huron that his or her house was empty (Steckley 1987a:21), an expression that probably referred to the inability of a matrilineal extended family to maintain its numbers. This failure had both social and economic consequences, since an aging and diminishing family was unable to play an effective role in the redistributive cycles upon which the prestige of its members depended.

Various taboos were observed during pregnancy. It was believed that if a pregnant woman looked at an animal her husband was stalking, the animal could not be taken. Likewise, if she entered the house of a sick person, that person would become worse. Yet the presence of a pregnant woman was thought essential for the successful extraction of an arrow, as practiced by the Wenro.

Women generally continued to work up to the time of their delivery and tried to be on their feet again as soon as possible afterwards. When a woman was about to give birth, a corner of the longhouse was partitioned off with a few skins. Some were attended by an old woman who performed the functions of a midwife; but more experienced women might deliver themselves. Women attempted not to cry out in childbirth for fear of being thought cowardly and failing to set a good example for others. Just as a man proved his courage in

Figure 18. Women carrying babies and load. One woman is wearing snowshoes. From Novae Franciae Accurata Delineatio.

battle, a woman proved hers by giving birth to a child. It was no easy task; physical anthropological and historical sources agree that a considerable number of women died in childbirth.

The mother pierced the ears of her newborn child with an awl or fishbone and stuck quills or some other small objects through the holes so they would not heal shut. Beads and other trinkets, including amulets, were hung about a child's neck. Some mothers made their children swallow grease as soon as they were born.

The Huron had a large supply of names available to give their children. Particular names were the property of different clan segments, and the custom was to give the child a clan name that was not in use at that time. When a man assumed another name upon inheriting a public office, his original one could be given to a newborn child. In this way, names were passed from generation to generation in particular matrilineages.

During the day, the baby was kept bound to a cradleboard about sixty centimeters long and thirty centimeters wide. Cradleboards were often decorated with paintings and strings of beads. The baby was swaddled in furs with an opening left for it to urinate through. In the case of a girl, a small corn leaf was used to carry away the urine without soiling the wrappings. A soft down made from cattails served as diapers. The cradleboard was often stood up on the floor of the longhouse. When the mother wished to carry the child with her, it was either hoisted onto her back by means of a tumpline or propped inside her dress in such a way that the child could look forward over her shoulder (Fig. 18). At night the child slept naked between its parents.

Women breastfed each child for two or three years, during which time they avoided sexual intercourse to ensure that they would not become pregnant. While the mother was still breastfeeding the child, she began to give it pieces of meat that she herself had masticated. If a mother died before the child was weaned, the father attempted to feed it by filling his mouth with corn soup and encouraging the child to swallow the liquid. Physical anthropological studies indicate that between the ages of two and four many children suffered from metabolic disturbances as a result of having to adapt to a nutritionally less adequate diet. There was also a high level of mortality at that time. This suggests that the Huron recognized the nutritional problems that were associated with feeding children on a corn-based diet and that, as a response, women set a high priority on nursing their children. Because of this, they did not rely on natural post-partum infecundability alone to ensure that a nursing mother would not become pregnant. This practice, combined with frequent separations of husbands and wives, resulted in the wide spacing of Huron births and the small size of Huron families.

One manifestation of the respect that Huron believed it was necessary to show to every individual was their refusal to use any form of physical punishment to discipline their children. This behavior was reinforced by the belief that public humiliation might lead a child to commit suicide. While children were sometimes verbally rebuked, they were allowed great freedom to do what they wanted. On the other hand, the subtle and often indirect patterns of praise and blame that pervaded all of Huron life made children anxious to conform to the behavioral patterns of their society.

Yet Huron children were not pampered. Young boys and girls frequently went about without clothing and even in winter ventured out of doors scantily clad. This was intended to harden them and ensure that they had robust constitutions in later life. From an early age boys were trained to use the bow and spent much time out of doors shooting arrows, learning to use the fish harpoon, and playing ball games or snow snake, which involved making a curved stick slide over the snow. These activities helped to forge strong friendships between boys of the same age, which in later life were often as important to them as those based on kinship. The training of girls was quite different. They learned to pound corn at an early age, and as they grew older, played games that taught them to perform household tasks. These activities kept them closely associated with their own household. When a girl reached puberty, she was not required to leave the house while she was menstruating, as were women in neighboring Algonkian societies. Henceforth, however, she cooked the food she ate separately during these periods. Women made small clay pots for this purpose.

At puberty young men went on a vision quest. One boy, about fifteen years old, went into the forest where he fasted, only drinking water for sixteen days. Then he heard a voice from the sky telling him to cease his fast, and an old man appeared to him. The old man announced that he was the boy's guardian spirit and that the boy would live to an old age and have four children. Then he offered the boy a piece of human flesh and a piece of bear fat. The boy ate the latter and thus became a successful hunter. In later years he stated that if he had eaten the human flesh that was presented to him in his vision, he would also have become a great warrior. Guardian spirits were expected to reappear in dreams and offer men advice throughout their lives. In times of danger or crisis, a man might also appeal to his guardian spirit for guidance.

MARRIAGE

Kissing and embracing in public was not permitted, even among young people. Huron, both married and unmarried, preferred to have sexual intercourse outside the settlement. This secured a degree of privacy that was not possible in their crowded longhouses. It may also have introduced a considerable amount of seasonal variation into the annual birth cycle.

In spite of such prudery, the Huron considered premarital sexual relations to be normal and engaged in them soon after puberty. Young people often had several sexual partners concurrently, and girls were as active as men in initiating these relations. The Huron shunned public displays of jealousy. Young men did not fight over girls and accepted that girls had the right to refuse their advances and to terminate an affair. Sometimes a young man and woman entered into a fairly longstanding, but informal, relationship, in which case the girl became known as the boy's companion. Such a relationship did not, however, preclude either partner from having sexual relations with other friends.

Young people avoided sexual intercourse with individuals they were not eligible to marry. The Huron were monogamous and did not marry any relative within three degrees of consanguinity on either the maternal or the paternal sides of their family. In addition, they were not supposed to marry any member of the same clan, even if that person belonged to some remote people. Brothers and sisters appear to have frequently married into the same families, and widows and widowers could marry their deceased spouse's brother or sister.

The Huron did not draw a simple distinction between being married and unmarried. Instead, they recognized various stages of experimentation and growing commitment between a man and a woman that did not culminate in a stable relationship until children were born.

While parents could not compel their children to marry, they played an important role in helping to arrange marriages. They often suggested a suitable girl to their son and, if he were agreeable, provided him with a present to offer her and approached the girl's parents to seek their support for the match. The consent of her parents was necessary for a marriage to be formalized. If these preliminaries met with success, the boy painted his face and, putting on the finest ornaments that he owned or could borrow, went to the girl and offered her his present. The latter might consist of a beaver robe or a wampum necklace. If she accepted the present, the boy spent a number of nights in succession with her. During this time the two had sexual intercourse but, unless they already knew each other well, did not speak to each other. After this, the girl could either reject her suitor or agree to marry him, but in either case she kept the present he had given her. Some girls displayed with pride the presents they had collected from numerous rejected suitors. If the girl agreed to marry, her family provided a feast to which the relatives and friends of the two families were invited. When all were assembled, the girl's father, or a master of ceremonies, announced the reason for the gathering and invited the guests to enjoy the feast. The woman now became the man's *atennonha*, or wife.

A girl's parents sometimes objected to a proposed marriage on the ground that the young man was not a good warrior, hunter, or fisherman and hence was incapable of looking after her. Young couples who were unable to obtain the permission of the girl's parents to marry sometimes ran away together, while well-disposed relatives tried to change her parents' minds. If a girl who had many lovers became pregnant, it was customary for each of these men to claim the child was his and for the girl to choose from among them the man that she wished to be her husband.

A marriage could be terminated at the desire of either partner. Prior to the birth of a child, infidelity and divorce seem to have been common, but afterwards married couples rarely separated. In spite of, or perhaps because of, the sexual freedom that had prevailed prior to this time, after children were born sexual relations between a husband and wife do not seem to have played a vital role in holding marriages together. Although adultery was not a legal offense, husbands did not indulge in it in any conspicuous fashion, although for several years after the birth of each child they were unable to have intercourse with their wives. Men spent long periods away from their wives each year, and marriages held together in spite of husbands being rendered permanently impotent as a result of illness. If couples who had been married a long time quarreled or separated, friends and relatives would intervene to reconcile them and save the marriage. In spite of the clan system, children sometimes lived with their fathers after a divorce, although young ones generally remained with their mothers.

In spite of the relative stability of mature marriages, even elderly Huron took the right of divorce seriously. Because she lived with her sisters and was partly supported by her brothers and brothers-in-law, a woman was never rendered totally dependent on her husband, while a man who was abused by his wife or her family had the option of returning to his mother's or sister's longhouse. It was therefore necessary for a husband and wife to treat each other with respect if their marriage was to succeed. In particular, the matrilineal bias of Huron family life protected women and children against abuse by men. There are no accounts of the mistreatment of Huron women in the seventeenth century, such as the French sometimes recorded concerning patrilocal native peoples.

6/Government and Law

The thousands of Huron who lived south of Matchedash Bay had evolved a social and political organization, as well as a subsistence economy, that permitted a far larger number of people to live together and cooperate than was the case among the Algonkian hunting bands that inhabited the Canadian Shield. By 1610, the Huron confederacy had expanded to embrace four peoples and over twenty communities. The largest settlements each contained as many as six clan segments and a total population of 1500–2000 people.

The confederacy effectively suppressed all blood feuds among its members. This permitted the Huron peoples to live side by side, to cooperate in their mutual defense, and to share a lucrative trade with the north. The unity of the Huron was not a temporary development brought about by the personality of an outstanding chief and likely to perish with him; instead it was founded on a carefully organized system of government that linked clan segments together to form communities, communities to form peoples, and peoples to form the confederacy. Through an elaborate series of councils, which began informally within each extended family and reached to the confederacy level, the activities of these groups were coordinated with one another in the general interest.

In spite of the size and complexity of the Huron confederacy, nothing about its organization shows any sign of being a radical departure from the egalitarian ideas about government that prevailed among the smaller-scale societies of the Lower Great Lakes region. The Huron confederacy had developed out of Iroquoian institutions that predated the adoption of a horticultural economy. Each household remained economically self-sufficient, and clan segments were willing to brook no interference in their internal affairs. Moreover, disagreements and disputes between clan segments, settlements, and even peoples were not uncommon. The Huron confederacy was not invested with any special powers to curb these tendencies; instead it attempted to resolve each crisis as it arose. Government, whether at the community, national, or confederacy level, strove to achieve a balance between the integrative and divisive forces that were inherent in Huron society. The confederacy respected the rights of its constituent clan segments, settlements, and peoples and elicited only enough support from these groupings to act for their common good. While the confederacy was a fragile structure built on an endless series of pragmatic compromises concerning specific issues, it was able to cope with the political challenges that confronted the Huron people prior to the arrival of the Europeans.

CHIEFS

All public offices were held by men. In part this was true because office holders had to visit other Huron communities and sometimes confront their counterparts among far-off and even hostile peoples—all of this being behavior that Huron considered appropriate for men rather than women. It also reflected the Huron belief that the focus of a woman's interest and power remained within her family and household.

The Huron term for chief (*yarihwa*) meant literally "he is great of voice." This does not mean that a chief was a person who gave orders. His primary duty was to announce decisions that were arrived at through a process of consensus that involved all the adult men and women of his group. Chiefs were not supposed to decide matters on their own and would not be obeyed if they did. Instead, they were expected to act as speakers or chairmen, first helping their own people come to an agreement about a course of action and then representing them in negotiations with other groups. No decision could be considered final until it had received the individual consent of every person who was expected to be bound by it. The ideal chief was not a man who argued with others or attempted to dominate them, but one who spoke softly and respected the opinions of others. It was also a fundamental rule of Huron society that any public respect accorded to a chief had to be reciprocated by a lavish distribution of food and other goods to his followers and anyone else he hoped to influence.

The Huron had two principal kinds of chiefs: *yarihwa endionhra* and *yarihwa ondoutayuehte*. The first were civil or peace chiefs who were concerned with problems of everyday life. They negotiated all foreign treaties, settled disputes, and arranged feasts, dances, and games. The second were war chiefs, who were concerned with waging war and killing witches. This division of responsibility represented the application to the political order of the distinction between peace and war, and more generally between reason and emotion, that played a major role in Huron thinking (Steckley 1978). The Huron believed that duties requiring quiet persuasiveness and the exercise of violence could not be successfully combined at the same time in the same person. Significantly, civil chiefs were the more important of the two. Each clan segment had two chiefs, one for peace and another for war. Thus, in large communities there were several chiefs of either sort, representing the various clan segments that composed the settlement.

Being a chief, especially a civil chief, required the expenditure of considerable time and wealth. They were expected to entertain their supporters as well as to provide hospitality for visitors. They also had to travel considerable distances to attend meetings, sometimes in very bad weather. The chief at whose house a meeting was held was obliged to provide food and entertainment for his visitors. This required him and his family to work harder than anyone else to produce the food that had to be given away to validate his public office. Likewise, most of the goods that chiefs received as presents or from their control of trade routes had to be given away to maintain the reputation for generosity without which a chief would have no support. The more influential a chief, which meant the larger were the number of people in whose name he spoke, the greater was the scale on which he had to provide feasts and give away exotic goods.

Civil chiefships were hereditary in particular lineages, the office passing from a chief to one of his brothers, and in the next generation to one of his sister's sons. While the hereditary nature of chiefship may have conflicted to some degree with the egalitarian ideals of Huron society, it served to minimize what might have been a potentially disruptive competition for public office among households and lineages. Chiefs were supported by the members of their clan segments but, unlike the situation among the Indians of the Northwest Coast, there appears to have been little overt status rivalry among them. The additional prestige that accrued to members of chiefly lineages was balanced by the need for members of those lineages to work extra hard to produce the food and other goods that a chief needed to give away to validate his status.

There was also no rule to determine which individual within a particular lineage should inherit an office. Instead, the lineage members, and in particular the older women of the lineage, selected the new chief. In doing so they considered the qualifications of each candidate to represent their clan segment. These included their intelligence, oratorical abilities, willingness to work, popularity, and above all their courage, as demonstrated by their past performance as warriors. Individuals who did not wish to play an active role in community life would refuse the offer of a chiefship. Chiefs who failed to perform the duties expected of them, and hence became objects of public complaint or ridicule, could be dismissed at any time by the women of their lineage.

The investiture of new chiefs usually took place at the annual meeting of the confederacy council. The main event of this ceremony was conferring on the new officeholder the ceremonial name of his predecessor, which henceforth replaced his previous personal name. The name of a man holding a particular office therefore remained unchanged from generation to generation. The Huron placed a strong emphasis on structural continuity in their political organization, which they considered to be more important than historical or genealogical considerations. A chief was expected not only to assume the name of his predecessor but also to exhibit similar personal qualities and to behave as much as possible like him.

Prior to an investiture, a magnificent feast was hosted by the newly selected chief's clan segment. The other chiefs who attended were well fed and provided with rich presents in order to win their support for the candidate. While each clan segment had the right to choose its own chief, the respect and goodwill of other chiefs were vital if he was to discharge the duties of his office successfully. Hence, the women of his lineage took care to select a candidate who would be acceptable to other chiefs and to win their support. After the new chief's appointment by his lineage was approved by the various chiefs of the confederacy, his new name was conferred on him. He was further identified with his predecessor by being symbolically drawn from the grave by the assembled chiefs. They then presented him with gifts on behalf of all the clan segments, communities, and peoples they represented. Each present was accompanied by an explanation of its symbolical meaning. Presents were given to draw the deceased from the grave, give him weapons to repel his enemies, and make the earth solid under his feet so that he would remain immovable during his tenure of office. Two women, probably the senior ones of his clan segment and lineage, were expected to attend the investiture; if they did not, this was believed to betoken misfortune for the officeholder.

New chiefs were presented with special insignia of office, which were passed from each officeholder to his successor and regarded as the most treasured objects in the country. These took the form of distinctive personal ornaments. Each chief also had a package of council sticks (*atsatonewai*), which functioned as his books and papers. They were mnemonic devices that served a purpose similar to strings and belts of wampum among the Iroquois, outlining the structure and seating plans of councils and the order in which speeches were to be made. Some of these sticks were buried with dead chiefs.

After the investiture, a second magnificent feast was held to celebrate what had happened. At this event old men recited Huron myths and traditions so that the young people could hear and remember them. These included the Huron account of the creation of the world. Following this celebration, a new chief often recruited young men to accompany him on a war expedition. His aim was to perform some daring exploit that would make it apparent that he had inherited the powers as well as the name of his predecessor. Hereafter, while civil chiefs might continue to join military expeditions, they left the expeditions' organization in the hands of the war chiefs.

The relatives of civil chiefs served them as assistants and counselors. At least one of these assistants was a deputy who frequently accompanied the chief and made public announcements in his name. An Iroquoian tendency to equate silence or soft-spokenness with power made it desirable for each civil chief to have a deputy who spoke publicly in his name. Hence, it was often difficult for strangers to determine who the actual chiefs were, and who were merely speaking for them. The various meetings and consultations by means of which a civil chief managed the affairs of his clan segment were attended by the representatives of the constituent households and lineages, as well as by all of the older men, whose opinions were considered seriously.

The office of war chief, while less prestigious than civil ones, was also hereditary within a particular lineage of each clan segment. War chiefs were often closely related to civil chiefs, and both offices normally seem to have been inherited within the same lineage. Some war chiefs held the office into old age and possibly for life. Others, who displayed desirable qualities, relinquished the war chief's position to a younger man, in order to accept a civil chiefship. While the duties of civil chiefs and war chiefs were clearly separated, in times of military crisis or when there was a panic about witchcraft the role of the war chief became more important and, for the duration of the emergency, war chiefs, with the support of younger men, might make decisions normally made by civil chiefs. As conditions returned to normal, civil chiefs regained their influence over the war chiefs, telling them when they could and could not wage war or seek out witches.

Only civil chiefs had seats on the national and confederacy councils. These met periodically and were responsible for maintaining order within the confederacy and peaceful relations with foreign peoples. War councils, which were held when needed to plan campaigns at the community, national, and confederacy levels, were attended by the war chiefs of the various clan segments. In Arontaen, the house of the leading war chief served as one meeting place for such councils. When greater security was desired, meetings were held at night in secret places in the forest. Sometimes the representatives of other nations at war with the Iroquois were invited to these meetings. In the late 1630s, the Jesuit missionaries were being asked to attend war councils as the representatives of the French.

Huron chiefs had no constitutional authority to coerce their followers or to force their will on anyone. Moreover, individual Huron were sensitive about their honor and intolerant of external constraints, and friends and relatives would rally to the support of someone who believed himself insulted by a chief. Overbearing behavior by a chief might, therefore, encourage a violent reaction and lead to conflicts within or between lineages. In the long run, chiefs who behaved arrogantly or foolishly tended to alienate support and would be deposed by their own lineages. The ideal Huron chief was a wise and brave man who understood his followers and won their support by means of his generosity, persuasiveness, and balanced judgement.

The enforcement of a chief's decision depended upon his securing the backing of public opinion and bringing this to bear against refractory individuals. The support that a skillful chief could muster in this fashion was quite considerable. The Jesuits recount that on one occasion when a young man struck a well-respected chief, the whole village rushed to the chief's aid and were restrained only with great difficulty from killing the young man on the spot. This reaction also reflected the commonly held belief that young men were irresponsible and had to be kept in line for the benefit of the community. By acquiring a good reputation, a chief was able to influence decision making to a considerable degree. To maintain such influence, he had to remain unstintingly generous and avoid any public display of arrogance or bad temper. Nor could he hope to retain public respect if he insulted or belittled anyone.

Many men who were neither civil chiefs nor war chiefs acquired a reputation for bravery, sagacity, or generosity which served to enhance their influence in the community. In later life, the opinions of these men came to carry considerable weight in the affairs of their village or people. While these prestigious individuals were known collectively as the Old Men, the more outstanding among them were called chiefs. The possibility of being recognized as an outstanding individual, even if no clan office was available, was a great encouragement to men to excel in subsistence activities, trade, and war.

COMMUNITY GOVERNMENT

The community (*yandata*) was a fundamental unit of Huron political organization. Its inhabitants interacted with each other on a daily basis, which created a special concern about each other's behavior not found at the national or confederacy level. It also involved an intimate concern with each other's physical and psychological welfare. Community members helped each other to build houses, aided those who were in distress, and shared the tasks involved in defending their settlement. They also participated in many feasts and collective rituals and joined societies whose membership crosscut their clan affiliations. In the large settlements, intermarriage among the different clan segments helped to forge additional bonds of community solidarity. Similar, although weaker, bonds served to connect smaller communities to larger neighboring towns.

The principal chiefs in each community were the civil and war chiefs of the clan segments, and in the larger towns there were a number of chiefs of each kind. Because these chiefs represented clan segments, they could not be removed from office except by their own clansmen. In principle, no chief was superior in rank to any other, but in practice one of the civil chiefs was recognized on a hereditary basis as the head chief, or spokesman, of the village. The size of the various clan segments also affected the influence exercised by different chiefs within each community.

The community councils were attended by the civil chiefs of the clan segments as well as by the Old Men. A council seems to have met frequently, perhaps even daily, to discuss local affairs. The meetings were normally held in the house of the head civil chief. Often there was little business to transact, and the group took on the characteristics of a social club. On more formal occasions, the head chief sat in front of the fire while the other chiefs and the Old Men formed a circle around it. When everyone had arrived, the doors of the house were closed and those present sat for a time quietly smoking their pipes (Fig.19). The smoke was believed to calm their minds and provide them with insight into the problems at hand. Then the head chief announced the business to be discussed in a loud, clear voice and those who had opinions to express did so. Men who did not speak but were believed to have something to contribute to the discussion were asked for their advice. Discussion continued until a consensus was reached. In practice that meant that proposals continued to be modified until all but a few who were involved supported a position, and those who did not decided that it was futile to continue the debate. While no one expected these hold-outs to join in whatever action was proposed, it was understood that they would not publicly oppose the decision

Figure 19. Chiefs smoking pipes at council meeting. From Novae Franciae Accurata Delineatio.

that had been made until a major shift in public opinion had occurred. Although anyone present could express an opinion, the chiefs and older men dominated the discussion. Any public announcements resulting from the deliberations of the council were made by the head chief or his deputy.

At these meetings matters that concerned the community as a whole were discussed. The decisions of the counselors covered many aspects of social life. It was they who arranged public feasts, dances, and lacrosse matches and who decided for whom special curing rites, requiring community participation would be performed. The latter work was facilitated because many of the men who sat on the community council also held important positions in the religious societies. In addition, the council undertook to see that no member of the community was in need and coordinated communal projects, such as building houses, erecting palisades, and deciding when the settlement should be relocated. All legal disputes between people who belonged to different clan segments within the community were adjudicated by the local council. Because all of the clan segments, as well as most of the larger and more important lineages, had members on the council, the interests of all the major groups received due consideration.

Legal disputes that arose between people living in different communities came to involve all the inhabitants of both settlements. While ideally such disputes may have been clan matters (Tooker 1964:52), clans (as distinguished from clan segments) were part of the ideal structure of Huron society, while communities were a concrete social reality. In most of these cases, clan segments living in the same community seem to have felt that they had more in common with each other than they did with segments of the same clan in other settlements. Hence when a clan segment found itself at odds with a clan segment in another settlement, the other clan segments in its community normally rallied to its defense and may even have contributed to reparations payments when these were necessary. Such action contributed greatly to the solidarity of the community. It is doubtful whether, with the exception of the clan segment itself, any other solidarity was considered more important.

Each village is reported to have had a stock of furs, wampum, and other goods that were at the disposal of its chiefs. These goods were obtained either as donations from members of the community or from other groups as part of peace treaties, exchanges of prisoners, and legal settlements. One of the chiefs was appointed to look after these goods, which were used for various purposes, such as seeking the support of other groups for waging war, offering public presents at the investiture of chiefs, and making the payments involved in settling disputes with other groups. If the supply of goods became exhausted, contributions were called for and, as it was considered evidence of public spiritedness to donate to this fund, such calls rarely went unanswered.

Occasionally there were general meetings attended by all the mature men of the community, which meant those who were approximately twenty-five years old and over. These assemblies were summoned by a special call. At these meetings announcements of special interest to the community were made and questions could be asked. No women or young men attended either the community council meetings or these general assemblies.

Yet, while public political activities were exclusively men's business, Huron women played an important role in political decision making. They not only appointed and could dismiss chiefs, but their views, and especially those of older women, were conveyed to the local council through the men who attended it. If these opinions were not listened to, the male participants could anticipate serious trouble when they returned to their longhouses. In general, women had a special interest in issues relating to community life, while men were more concerned with relations between communities. Huron women were the guardians of family and community traditions, while men, who spent more time visiting far off peoples, were more used to, and tolerant of, cultural differences. Yet men and women both had a significant input into most discussions of public policy. For example, chiefs had to obtain permission from women before they could take teenage boys away from the community on trading or military expeditions. This gave women a significant voice in the conduct of foreign affairs. Because of the Huron belief that silence denoted strength, and the inability of any council decision to bind any person contrary to his or her own assent, even the exclusion of women from public political activity did not necessarily imply political inferiority. As in many other aspects of their life, the Huron recognized that men and women had different interests but gave each other the freedom to control what was of interest to them.

NATIONAL GOVERNMENT

Because the Tahontaenrat all inhabited a single settlement, their community and national governments were probably identical. Each of the other Huron nations or peoples had a council that was apparently made up of the chiefs of the clan segments from its various communities. One of these was recognized as the principal chief and spokesman for the entire people, who on ceremonial occasions were often referred to by their chief's official name. The word *hennondecha* also meant, alternatively, chief, people, and the district where a people lived. Like head chiefs at the community level, the principal chiefship of a people appears to have been hereditary in a single lineage. Foreign groups had to obtain the permission of this chief if they wished to cross his people's territory. This was usually granted in return for a donation to the national treasury.

Sagard reports that the principal chief of the Attignawantan was called Awendaon and that he lived in Khinonascarant. In 1636 Annenkhiondik was said to be the chief of the Attignawantan. He lived in Ossossané, which was the largest Attignawantan settlement. Awendaon (later Aennons) remained the most important chief among the northern Attignawantan, and the rivalry between him and Annenkhiondik, which may have been a longstanding one, seems to reflect the fundamental division between the northern and southern Attignawantan that we noted previously. Endahiakonk, the principal chief of the Attigneenongnahac, was also the head chief of Teanaostaiaé, which was their largest community. The principal chief of the Arendahronon was Atironta. Because he was the chief of the first Huron people to encounter the French, all of the Huron regarded him and his successors as the special allies of the French.

The principal chiefs of the various Huron peoples were not like European heads of state. Although the members of a particular people shared a common territory and had common traditions, they viewed themselves politically as a collection of clan segments. They were willing to accept the idea that, because of its size or for historical reasons, one clan segment could be more influential than another and recognized that the chief of one such group had the right to act as spokesman for the entire people. They did not believe, however, that this gave a chief the right to intervene in the internal affairs of any clan segment other than his own. This insistence on the right of clan segments to manage their own affairs provided each chief, however small his clan segment, with a solid and inalienable basis of independence in his dealings with other chiefs.

The power of the principal chief was also limited because each of the chiefs on the national council was recognized as being responsible for some particular matter pertaining to the government of the people or confederacy. These charges were seen as inherent in the office itself and were passed on from generation to generation. For example, a northern Attignawantan chief named Tsondechwanwan was entrusted with all matters pertaining to the foreign groups his people visited by water along the shores of Lake Huron. Messages to these groups were usually sent in his name. A similar situation was found among the Iroquois, where particular sachems, or council chiefs, were held responsible for those duties that had been assigned to their predecessors at the founding of the league.

It appears that any chief could call a council meeting about a problem falling within his particular sphere of concern. Most meetings, however, were summoned by the principal chief and met in his longhouse. Some chiefs had to travel considerable distances to attend these councils, which were held during the winter as well as in the warm weather. When a meeting was decided upon, messengers were sent to inform the chiefs about it. Sometimes young men served as messengers, but if the situation was a particularly serious one, older men were sent, as their word would carry more weight. One of the important duties of these councils was to help settle disputes between members of different communities belonging to the same people. If the representatives of the clan segments or communities that were involved failed to mediate the dispute, the council would try to work out a solution. It also discussed matters of concern to the confederacy as a whole with an eye to formulating proposals that would best serve the interests of a particular people. Often the views of the four peoples concerning foreign policy differed radically. These councils, like the community ones, did not have any authority to compel clan segments or individuals to obey their decisions; that required winning the assent of the chiefs of the clan segments, who in turn had to gain the support of their followers. For this reason issues were discussed until a consensus, or near consensus, was reached. In general, there was less pressure for groups to reach an agreement at this level than at the community one, since the parties involved were geographically more dispersed. Moreover, the number of matters that had to be decided was much smaller. When a request was made to such a council, it was usually accompanied by presents that were put into the national treasury. This was used much like the stocks of goods belonging to clan segments and communities.

THE HURON CONFEDERACY

The formal machinery of government on the confederacy level functioned much the same as it did on the national one. The confederacy council appears to have been made up of the civil chiefs who sat on the various national councils. Thus, the chiefs who made up the confederacy council probably represented most, if not all, of the Huron clan segments. The two founding peoples of the Huron confederacy were accorded ceremonial seniority by comparison with the Arendahronon and Tahontaenrat. Each pair of peoples addressed each other as brother and sister and the other pair as cousins. The Attignawantan, because of their size, dominated council meetings in a way that none of the five tribes ever dominated those of the Iroquois. The chief who presided over them was an Attignawantan. In the 1630s this chief was very old and blind.

An unresolved question is the status of the Tahontaenrat, the last and probably the smallest of the peoples to join the confederacy. The Jesuits state that only three peoples were represented at the one confederacy council meeting they described in detail. It is possible that this number is a mistake or that for some reason the Tahontaenrat were not present at this particular meeting. It may also be, however, that while the Tahontaenrat had been admitted to the confederacy about 1610, they had still not been assigned official seats on the confederacy council. Their position would have been similar to that of the Tuscarora who joined the Iroquois league in the eighteenth century. The Tuscarora were treated exactly the same as the other Iroquois peoples, except that they were not permitted to have their chiefs made official members of the council, since the Iroquois were unwilling to disrupt its traditional roster of members. Instead, they were represented by the Oneida. While the Huron were not equally inflexible in the early part of the seventeenth century, as their admission of the Arendahronon shows, it may have taken time for a small group, such as the Tahontaenrat, to be seated on the confederacy council. In the 1630s they may still have been attending as observers.

The principal meeting of the confederacy council occurred each year in the spring and lasted several weeks. At this time new chiefs were installed and war feasts were held. Between council meetings many feasts and celebrations took place and numerous presents were exchanged. The main function of these meetings appears to have been to strengthen the bonds of the confederacy by bringing together the chiefs of the various clan segments and providing them with an opportunity to reaffirm their friendship and discuss problems of mutual interest. Other meetings were held as issues of importance to the whole confederacy arose.

The latter meetings could be called by any confederacy chief who, after consulting his community and national councils, decided that a matter had arisen that was important enough to deserve general consideration. He then sent out messengers requesting the other chiefs, especially those whom the matter concerned the most, to gather in his village on a particular day to discuss it. The causes for these special meetings varied. One was held in the course of an epidemic to consider charges that the Jesuits were sorcerers who were causing the Huron to die. Another was called after some chiefs had slain a French workman who was employed by the Jesuits. Disputes arising out of the murder of a member of one Huron people by a member of another might disrupt the league, and these were subjects for discussion by the confederacy council. If a Huron murdered a member of a friendly people, compensation was offered in the name of the entire confederacy by the representatives of each of the eight Huron clans. No doubt the chiefs who presented these gifts were all members of the confederacy council, and in most cases a general meeting had been required to discuss what course of action was necessary.

Impending Iroquois attacks and matters of foreign policy that required quick decisions were also causes for special meetings of the council. These meetings usually took place at the house of the chief who had called them, often at night. If it was summer and greater secrecy was required, the chiefs might assemble in the forest. Houses where meetings were held were lined with mats and fir branches for the chiefs to sit on. In earlier times each chief was said to have brought his own faggots to put in the fire, but in the historical period the women of the household tended the fires, although they did not stay for the meetings.

At meetings of the confederacy council, the chiefs from each community and their deputies sat together so that they could consult one another. The Attignawantan sat on one side of the longhouse, the remaining peoples on the other. If someone was absent, the chiefs discussed whether the meeting should begin without this person being present. Usually the decision depended on whether the items to be discussed were of particular concern to him. After this, the chiefs who had come from other communities were welcomed, and thanksgiving was offered that they had arrived safely, without having fallen into a stream or been attacked by enemy raiders. Tobacco was distributed to the more prominent members of the council, who in turn shared it with the members of their delegations. Then, as at the community meetings, there was an interval of silence during which the counselors smoked their pipes and composed their thoughts.

After the subject of the meeting was announced, the representatives of each people and community were asked their opinion on the matter, and they consulted among themselves deciding what their reply should be. Then their spokesmen gave their answer, slowly and distinctly, repeating the subject under discussion and summarizing what had been said before to show that they understood it clearly. The formality of the proceedings helped to encourage politeness, moderation, and good humor, which were considered essential to the conduct of a meeting. Violent outbursts were rare and strongly disapproved of, even if the issue was a hotly disputed one. Each speaker ended with the words "that is my thought on the subject." The assembly responded with a *haau*. If the person had spoken to their liking, the *haau* was given much more forcefully. Issues often were discussed late into the night. While the more junior participants in the council might leave, the clan segment chiefs stayed until the end.

The language used in these councils was different from everyday speech and had a special name, *akwaentonch*. Some technical and archaic words were used only in council speech, and various metaphors, circumlocutions, and other rhetorical devices were employed to embellish the discourse that were not used in everyday speech. Speeches were also delivered in a high-pitched and quavering voice. This made it especially difficult even for foreigners who understood the Huron language to follow what went on at these councils.

REPRESSION OF BLOOD FEUDS

The Huron confederacy was constructed out of local clan groupings which refused to surrender any control over their internal affairs to a higher body. Action at the village, national, and confederacy levels required agreement among the clan segments that made up these levels, just as a chief's power to act depended upon securing the approval of his followers. Under these circumstances, the construction of the confederacy and its continued functioning were feats of no mean order. Strong centrifugal forces were present which at a time of crisis or dissension could threaten the functioning and very existence of the confederacy. These forces were a source of great anxiety to the Huron, who strove to minimize their effects. Nowhere are their efforts to do this more apparent than in the sphere of law.

The Huron recognized four main classes of crime: murder and its lesser equivalents wounding and injury, theft, witchcraft, and treason. The most potentially disruptive of these was murder. Murder placed an obligation upon the kinsmen of the slain person to avenge the killing by slaying the murderer or one of his relatives. That, in turn, could lead to a prolonged blood feud between the clan segments, communities, or peoples to which the two parties belonged, with disastrous consequences for the confederacy. Possibly, when all the peoples of the region had lived in small groups and depended mainly on hunting and gathering, blood revenge was the usual way of avenging murders. With the growth of large communities and confederacies, the disruptive effects of such disputes must have become intolerable, and new ways of dealing with murder had to be devised. The importance that the Huron placed on the suppression of blood feuds is shown by Brébeuf's comment that blood revenge was considered the most reprehensible of all crimes—far worse than murder itself.

While every effort was made to suppress blood feuds, no attempt was made to redefine the traditional rights of the groups involved. Peoples and clan segments theoretically retained the right of blood revenge, but it was agreed that, in practice, blood feuds within the Huron confederacy would be settled by the group to which the murderer belonged paying reparations to the kinspeople of his victim. Murder continued to be viewed as a matter concerning the respective social groups of the murderer and his victim, and society as a whole did not presume to pass judgement on any individual for the crimes he (most murderers seem to have been men) had committed. The personal treatment that he received was a matter for his own clan segment and lineage to decide. Normally it took the form of rebukes and insults rather than any kind of physical punishment. All the members of a clan segment shared the cost of paying reparations for a murder committed by one of their group. They also shared in the distribution of reparation payments if a member of their segment was killed by an outsider. If kinsmen resorted to blood revenge, not only were all of their segment's rights to receive compensation forfeited, but they themselves were regarded as murderers and their segment was required to pay the regular indemnities for their actions to the family of their victim. Only if, after prolonged discussion, the clanspeople of the murderer refused to pay compensation did the relatives of the murdered person have the right to take up arms against them. This happened only rarely.

The Huron claimed that in earlier times, in addition to the compensation his clan segment, village, or people had to pay, a murderer was compelled to lie in a cage directly under the rotting corpse of his victim until the latter's relatives gave him permission to leave, possibly in return for still more compensation. This custom was practiced by no Huron group in the historical period, and possibly it had belonged to a particular people, or community, who had given it up after they had joined the confederacy. Even in this case, however, although the family of the murdered man had the murderer in their power, they had to stop short of killing him and thereby giving his relatives cause to avenge his death.

The precise constitutional mechanisms for settling blood feuds are not always clear, nor is it certain that every murder was resolved in exactly the same fashion. If a murder was committed within a clan segment, it was treated as a matter of concern to that group alone, although payments were probably made from one lineage to another. If a member of one clan segment killed a member of another within the same community, the settlement was negotiated by the local council. If the murderer and his victim lived in different communities, the affair was mediated by the two community councils. If a settlement proved difficult to arrange, the case became a matter of concern to an entire people, and their national council exercised its good offices to try to reach a solution. The same was true of the confederacy council if the murderer and murdered person belonged to different peoples or a Huron and someone from a friendly foreign group were involved.

The importance of clan ties in legal settlements is indicated by the role that was played by the sisters, uncles (mother's brothers), and nephews (sister's sons) of murder victims in avenging their deaths. When the Attignawantan were struck by an epidemic after some of them murdered the French trader Etienne Brûlé, they assumed that his sister or uncle was practising witchcraft against them. Likewise, the Jesuits speak of nephews rather than sons accusing them of witchcraft when various Huron died. Lalemant stated that a niece was a surer support for a man than were his own children. The responsibility of a clan segment to defend one of its members did not cease even if that person was married and living elsewhere. A woman's relatives were entitled to claim reparations for her murder even though she resided in a different settlement.

The amount of compensation varied according to the sex and status of the murdered person. If a chief or Old Man was slain, the compensation was greater than for a younger man, and significantly more was required for the slaying of a woman than of a man. The reasons given for the latter difference were that women were less able to defend themselves and more valuable to their families because of their reproductive capacity. It also reflected the matrilineal bias of Huron family organization. The average reparation for a man was about thirty presents and for a woman forty, each of the presents having the approximate value of a beaver robe. If the dispute were between the Huron and some foreign group with whom they traded on a regular basis, the amount was even greater; however, the burden on any one individual was less because the compensation was paid by the confederacy as a whole rather than by the members of a single community or clan segment. Those receiving compensation had the right to reject any present that they believed was unworthy and to demand another in its place. After the amount of compensation was settled by the groups concerned, a bundle of sticks was presented to the murderer's people, community, or clan segment, indicating the number of presents that were required. The chiefs divided these sticks among the various groups involved and exhorted their followers to provide the necessary goods. It does not appear that the household of the murderer was asked to contribute more than any other. Clanspeople and fellow villagers often vied with each other to demonstrate their public spiritedness in helping a murderer's family.

These presents were transferred at a formal ceremony which often lasted several days. They were divided into two groups. The first set of presents was intended to make peace with the victim's relatives and to assuage their desire for revenge. The second was given to ransom the murderer, who had to attend the ceremony. The latter gifts were tied to a pole placed above the murderer's head. Each present had its own name, which expressed the symbolic act that it was intended to accomplish. The first two expressed the regret of the murderer and his wish to restore the dead person to life. Others were given to restore the unity of the country and to console and remove the bitterness from the hearts of the dead person's relatives. Then a series of presents was given representing the things the deceased had used during his life, such as his robe, canoe, and bow and arrows. At the end of the ceremony, the relatives of the dead person gave some small presents to the group paying compensation as evidence that the murderer was forgiven and the matter closed.

In this way, the Huron were able to curb murders without employing the death penalty or in any way directly punishing the person responsible. By holding peoples, settlements, and especially clan segments responsible for the behavior of their members, they were able to secure order within the confederacy without interfering with the traditional rights of these groups. Since all the members of a group stood to lose through the misbehavior of a single member, it was in everyone's interest to bring pressure to bear on troublesome individuals to behave properly. Someone who repeatedly committed crimes gradually alienated his clanspeople, and there was the danger that his close relatives might take reprisals against him. One woman is reported to have been killed by her brother because she was an incorrigible thief; hence, there is no doubt that a pathological murderer would have been dealt with in the same way. Yet the most effective punishment inflicted on most murderers was the realization that what they had done had resulted in public humiliation and economic loss to their group. This involved them in a moral debt that could be repaid only if henceforth they behaved properly. In this way, the network of social relations that linked the Huron people together served to control its members.

In arranging for reparations payments, the chiefs acted as referees. One of their duties was to try to determine who had actually committed the murder. This was not easy, since murderers often killed their victims in the fields or while traveling between villages and tried to make the killings appear as if they had been done by Iroquois raiders. Other murders were planned so that suspicion would fall on other Huron. In one case a man, who was probably mentally disturbed, robbed his father-in-law and carried the loot to his mother's house in another village. In accordance with Huron custom, his father-in-law and his supporters went to the mother's house and carried off everything they found there. The thief then murdered his own brother in such a fashion that the blame for it fell on his father-in-law, and he and his community were forced to pay compensation. Later a girl confessed that she had witnessed the murder, and the father-in-law was cleared of the accusation.

OTHER CRIMES

Wounding was a less serious offense than murder. It was compensated with presents that varied in value according to the seriousness of the injury and the status of the person who had been attacked; an assault on a chief being treated as an affront to his whole clan segment. There is no evidence that wounding as a result of deliberate assault was differentiated from accidental wounding. Wounds inflicted by one Huron on another as the result of a hunting accident were compensated in the same way as if they had been caused deliberately. When the French who accompanied Champlain went hunting with the Huron in 1615, a Huron was accidentally wounded as a result of wandering into their line of gunfire. The affair was quickly settled, in the traditional Huron manner, by the French giving him presents. Ordinary cases were adjudicated by the community chiefs and the compensation was paid either by the offender or by his community. If the person who was injured was a prominent individual from another community, not only did he receive compensation but a feast was given in his honor. Moreover, his assailant was severely criticized by his own community.

Public disapproval and condemnation of thieves provided the best protection for an individual's personal possessions. Huron frequently stole from foreign groups with whom they were not on particularly friendly terms and were praised for doing so. Such behavior was regarded as analogous to stealing valuable goods when raiding enemy territory. A Huron who lacked some necessity would be little criticized for taking what he needed from another Huron, especially if that person had more than he or she needed of that item. It was accepted that the owner should have offered it to someone who needed it without being asked. The ability of the Huron to manufacture most of the things that they needed and the extent to which exotic goods were redistributed in religious rituals and as evidence of generosity, caused the Huron to be less possessive of personal property than Europeans were. A more important concern was to minimize the disruptive consequences of quarrels that might arise as a result of accusations of theft.

In part they did this by defining theft very narrowly. It was viewed as the removal of goods from an individual by force or from inside a longhouse without permission. A person was legally entitled to claim as his or her own anything that was found lying about unattended. A case described by the Jesuits provides an interesting example of the application of this rule. A woman temporarily left a valued shell necklace in the fields, where it was found and claimed by a neighbor. When the case was taken before the community chiefs, they pronounced that the woman who had taken the necklace was legally entitled to keep it, but added that if she did not want people to think badly of her she should return it, perhaps in return for a small present as evidence of the original owner's appreciation. This case provides an interesting example of the working of the Huron legal system, because it demonstrates not only the regard that was shown for abstract rules but also how those rules were interpreted to produce a socially more satisfactory solution. In order to protect their valuables, both from theft and from fire, the Huron hid them in bark-lined caches dug into the floors of their houses, or else carried them around with them.

The Huron did not impose any fines or penalties on a thief personally, and they did not permit a man from whom goods had been stolen to reclaim them without first inquiring how the person in whose possession they were found had come by them. If that person claimed that he had gotten them from someone else, he was expected to give the person's name, and the original owner was required to question that person in turn. A refusal to answer constituted an admission of guilt. Shamans were sometimes hired to uncover a thief by supernatural means, but their methods were widely believed to work only if the thief was present in the audience and betrayed himself by showing fear. Once a person was able to prove who had robbed him, he had the right to go with his relatives to the thief's longhouse and try to carry away by force everything of value inside. Normally, not even members of the same clan segment or lineage would come to the assistance of such an extended family. Thus, the household of a man who had stolen very little might be despoiled of everything it possessed. Fear of this happening put pressure on each household to enforce the good behavior of its members.

To prevent this rule from being used as an excuse for one extended family to rob another, it was required that an accusation of theft had to be supported with evidence before action could be taken. Another example of the Huron concern to prevent brawling between families and a deterioration of public order was the rule that permitted the owner of a trade route to despoil anyone using it illegally, provided that person had not yet returned to his community. Afterward the wronged party might complain, but no action could be legitimately taken to punish the person who had used the route illegally.

Two crimes were regarded as deserving punishment by death. In theory, witches caught casting spells could be slain by anyone without fear of penalty or condemnation. Traitors who sold information to the enemy or conspired with them to harm their own people could also be killed. While the latter were usually slain on the orders of the chiefs, the Huron maintained that anyone had the right to slay a witch. Moreover, a sick person's dream, a rumor, or being seen alone in the woods was enough to arouse suspicions of witchcraft in some people's minds. In times of crisis, when tensions ran high, and especially when diseases threatened Huron communities, the fear of witches reached crisis proportions. Unless it was subject to some form of social control, the right to kill witches could have degenerated into a mere excuse for killing people and have had extremely disruptive consequences. In the next chapter we shall examine how this fear was kept under control.

7/Power in Huron Society

THE IDEAL OF INDEPENDENCE

We have already noted strongly egalitarian tendencies in Huron society. These manifested themselves in two ways: in a refusal to tolerate any one section of society possessing notably more wealth than another, and in the refusal of any individual or group to obey the commands of another. While individuals and families were prepared to work hard, they did not seek to accumulate large amounts of goods for their own use but rather so they could give them away. No Huron family was allowed to go hungry or to be without shelter and other basic necessities, so long as other people in the community had any possessions to share with them. Even if exotic goods were originally obtained by a small number of traders and chiefs, they were widely distributed throughout Huron society in religious rituals and as part of chiefly efforts to win social approval and political support. In theory, and to a large degree in practice, leadership involved repeatedly securing the consent of followers and thus remained highly personal. The Huron expected chiefs and their families to reciprocate for the public support they received by producing and distributing more resources than anyone else.

Like many other small-scale societies, the Huron valued conformity to the extent that a man or woman was judged very largely according to his or her ability to live up to seemingly unchanging ideals about socially appropriate behavior. Idiosyncratic behavior was strongly discouraged, except in a few restricted and well-defined social contexts. The Huron greatly feared dishonor and reproach, both as individuals and as groups; hence gossip and public criticism were powerful factors making for conformity in Huron life.

However, it is a fallacy to equate intolerance of idiosyncratic behavior with a lack of respect for the dignity of individuals. The Huron strongly objected to individuals or groups overtly trying to coerce anyone into behaving contrary to his or her expressed wishes. If such coercion came from outside a person's lineage or clan segment, it was an affront to that person's clanspeople as well as to the individual. While men and women attempted to live up to the ideals of their society, they remained highly sensitive of their honor and personal independence in their relationships with others.

We have already seen evidence of this independence in the behavior of Huron men. The ideal man was a brave warrior who was self-reliant, intolerant of restraint, and indifferent to the pain that others might try to inflict on him. These values were inculcated into boys at an early age, and Huron men continued to test their courage and self-reliance throughout life. They took pride in their ability to provide meat and skins for their families, spent much of their lives in activities that took them away from their homes and villages, and frequently exposed themselves to personal danger.

The Huron showed equal concern for the dignity of women and children. Women freely expressed their opinions on a wide variety of topics and, especially in their homes, often joined together to behave contrary, or without reference to, their husbands' wishes. Divorce was as easy for women as it was for men, and because they lived in matrilineal households, it was relatively easy for them to defend their collective rights. While women may have been less sensitive about their personal honor than men were, an examination of legal actions and curing feasts suggests that there was no less public concern for their rights and well-being than for those of men. The Huron refusal to use corporal punishment to train children reflected their view that a child was already a person with rights and needs of his or her own, as opposed to the European view that a child was an unformed being that must be molded and constrained to become an acceptable adult (Tooker 1964:124).

The lifelong right of an individual to be free from overt constraint is also evident in Huron law, where it was reinforced by the jealousy with which Huron lineages and clans guarded their privileges and independence. Huron law did not permit either society as a whole or single chiefs to punish individuals for most forms of misconduct. Even murder was punished through the payment of compensations not by the murderer, but by his clan segment or community, to the clan segment or community of his victim. Individuals who habitually caused trouble for their families were subjected to informal but powerful sanctions, and in rare instances, immediate kin might have to kill socially dangerous misfits. Generally, however, the assumption of responsibility for individuals by the group served to reinforce their ties with society at precisely the same time that psychological pressures to conform were being applied to them; hence, the psychologically punitive aspects of these sanctions were muted. The aim of Huron legal action was not to punish the offender but to awaken in him a sense of responsibility toward those who were closest to him. Ultimately this concern manifested itself in the individual agreeing to conform to the norms of Huron society of his or her own free will.

SUICIDE

Huron sensitivity was reflected in a high suicide rate. People took their own lives either because of excessive grief over the death of relatives or close friends or because of humiliations they had suffered at the hands of others. One man committed suicide because his wife had divorced him, another because the heavy losses that he had incurred while gambling made him ashamed to face his relatives. Parents tended to indulge their children, fearing that they might kill themselves if they were treated severely. Methods for committing suicide included hanging oneself and eating the poisonous root of the water hemlock (*Cicuta maculata*) Emetics were known that could be used as an antidote to this poison. Prisoners who committed suicide to avoid torture were regarded as especially contemptible cowards and a disgrace to their people.

PRIVILEGE

Even if the ideals underlying Huron society were largely egalitarian ones, we must enquire how completely they were realized in everyday life and whether there were alternative ones. There are numerous aspects of Huron life which suggest the possible existence of institutionalized as well as informal inequality in Huron society. The most important political offices, not only within clan segments but also at the national and confederacy level, were hereditary within particular lineages, and chiefs had close relatives as their deputies and counselors. Chiefs and their families also lived in longhouses that were more spacious than those of other people. These households, and ones whose members had acquired special prominence as a result of their generosity and success as traders and warriors, enjoyed privileges that were denied to others. Community chiefs would sanction village-wide curing ceremonies only for members of such families, judging their sickness alone to be of public importance. These were also the families that received prisoners for adoption and torture to compensate them for their losses to the enemy.

Chiefs were also the recipients of many outward signs of respect, although there were no forms of address to distinguish them from any other older men. They were invited to many feasts, both in their own community and elsewhere, and were presented with the best servings of food. Chiefs also controlled particular trade routes, with leading chiefs controlling the most important ones. Their permission was required before anyone else could legitimately trade along these routes, and because presents were required to secure this permission, chiefs profited from their control of them. They are also reported to have reserved the best part of public presents for themselves. This implies that they appropriated larger shares of reparations payments and other legal settlements for themselves than they passed on to their followers. The Jesuits claimed that older and more important chiefs took advantage of the ritual redistribution of furs at the Feast of the Dead in order to appropriate a large number of these furs for themselves. Likewise, it is reported that when a Huron or a stranger wanted to obtain some favor, he offered presents to the chiefs "at whose beck and call all the rest moved."

While all of this suggests that chiefs and their families constituted an economically as well as politically privileged group in Huron society, care must be taken not to misinterpret this evidence. If Huron chiefs and their families were the recipients of captives and special curing ceremonies, this was true because their generosity and hospitality, supported largely by the hard work of family members, created a social indebtedness that obliged other members of the community to do more for their welfare than they did for that of other families. Prisoner sacrifices and curing ceremonies also involved the lavish distribution of hospitality by the family for whom these rituals were performed. None of this behavior violated the basic principle that public honor and attention had to be reciprocated by the production and distribution of material goods, an arrangement that encouraged not only hard work but also the equitable distribution of resources. Chiefs' houses were larger than those of other people because they served as guest houses and community meeting places, with most of the cost of entertainment being borne by the chiefs' families. They were not more elaborately constructed or furnished than were other houses.

Chiefs may have used their control over trade routes and reparations presents to acquire large amounts of goods. Yet there is no evidence that they sought to retain extraordinary amounts of this material for themselves or their families. Instead they had to distribute these goods liberally in order to maintain their prestige. A chief and his family who acquired a reputation for stinginess, or anything less than generosity, would soon lose their influence. Chiefs and their lineages had to work hard to maintain their privileged position, and even the exotic goods that chiefs accumulated had in large part to be given away for political and ceremonial reasons.

Autocracy and acquisitiveness were also held in check by the factionalism that was endemic among the Huron. For a community or people to hold together, it was necessary that the constituent clan segments treat each other with respect. While generosity promoted good will, greediness or arrogant behavior produced political strife that would have quickly torn the higher levels of consensus-based Huron political structures apart; the splitting apart of large communities indicates it sometimes did. In order to avoid this danger and to enhance their influence, chiefs and their clan segments sought to demonstrate their generosity to the other clan segments that made up the Huron confederacy. If chiefs were acquisitive in particular situations, it was to enable them to be generous on the numerous occasions when such behavior was required. Distributions of food and exotic goods were essential features of public feasts, major building projects, life-cycle ceremonies, curing rituals, community and personal religious celebrations, ritual friendships, the settlement of disputes, and the conduct of diplomacy. In all of these situations chiefs and their families were expected to be outstandingly generous, to the point where they were left with little more, and possibly sometimes less, for their own use than anyone else.

The limited power of chiefs is evident in their conduct of foreign diplomacy, which was often characterized by the favoring of different policy options among clan segments and between the civil chiefs and young men. Certain chiefs carried on negotiations with foreign groups, particularly ones with whom the Huron were at war, without informing other chiefs of the nature of these discussions. Often the talks concerned the release of prisoners. These discussions were generally supported by clan segments who had members being held prisoner by the Iroquois and were opposed by clan segments that did not. In the 1640s the Arendahronon, many of whom had relatives being held captive by the Iroquois, were anxiously negotiating with the Iroquois, but the Attignawantan were opposed to these talks. Sometimes, if negotiations were desired, an important prisoner was freed in such a way that it looked as if he had escaped. Fear of public opinion being rallied against them, especially if the negotiations failed, appears to have made chiefs highly secretive about such activities. The main objections to their actions were likely to have been raised by young men who were anxious to win reputations as warriors. Probably only the more important chiefs and their advisors knew the identity of the contacts that the Huron maintained among neutral and hostile peoples. These contacts were presented with gifts drawn from the communal funds that were at the disposal of the various chiefs. This suggests that these chiefs were not particularly accountable to their followers or to each other for the use of such funds. It does not, however, constitute evidence of their abuse of power, since when they did this they probably had to replenish these funds from their own resources.

WITCHCRAFT AND SOCIAL EQUALITY

Hard work, generosity, and economic equality, as well as individual conformity to other social norms, were maintained by a series of positive and negative sanctions, which constrained Huron behavior, although never directly. Those who lived up to the ideals of Huron society were rewarded with public esteem and influence. Those who did not, including chiefs, became the objects of censorious gossip and even public ridicule. The most powerful mechanism of social control in Huron society was, however, their belief in witchcraft.

The Huron feared becoming the victims of witchcraft practiced either consciously or unconsciously by men and women who envied or hated them. While anyone's ill will was potentially dangerous, and therefore something to be avoided, the Huron especially feared individuals who were thought to be skilled in the use of magical spells, which had either been taught to them secretly by kinspeople or been revealed by malevolent spirits in the form of dreams. With the aid of these spirits, such men and women were able to inflict injuries on those they disliked, or even kill them. The Huron agreed that witches (*oki ontatechiata* "those who kill by spells") had, by repudiating the normal bonds of reciprocity that held Huron society together, forfeited any rights to protection, even by their closest relatives. They were the secret enemies of their people in the same way that the Iroquois were their declared enemies. Hence, when they were discovered, they deserved to be treated in the same fashion.

Witches could cause their victims to suffer misfortunes, including loss of belongings, injuries, and housefires. The most common manifestation of witchcraft was, however, physical illness. Such diseases did not respond to curing by natural methods and could be diagnosed either by a shaman or by sick persons having the cause of their misfortune revealed to them in dreams. Shamans, called *ontetsens* or *atetsens*, specialized in treating these diseases. The illness was assumed to be caused by the witch making a foreign object, such as a tuft of hair, nail parings, an animal's claw, a piece of leather, a pebble, or some sand, enter a person's body. It was believed that in order to do this the charm had to be rubbed with the flesh of an *angont*, a powerful horned serpent spirit that lived under the ground or in the water, and which brought disease, death, and misfortune. The shaman's aim was to remove this charm by giving the patient an emetic to induce vomiting, sucking the charm from the patient's body, or extracting it with the point of a knife without leaving an incision. One shaman shook a man who suffered from a high fever and made sand fly from all parts of his body. Sometimes as many as twenty different charms were "removed." If an individual did not recover after the treatment was finished, it was assumed that charms remained in the person's body which were impossible to find and might eventually kill their victim.

The Huron believed that the principal motivation for witchcraft was jealousy. Thus, if a man had been especially successful in hunting, fishing, or trading or if a family's harvest had been particularly good, they felt threatened by witchcraft. One way to attempt to avert trouble was for an individual to share the fruits of his good fortune with as many people as possible. Yet even slight and unintended offenses might cause a witch to seek to harm someone; hence the most generous individual was in danger. The Huron feared witches to such a degree that extended families who felt threatened sometimes moved to another community in the hope of avoiding their displeasure.

The Huron maintained that witches should be put to death, and that if they were caught performing an act of sorcery they could be slain by anyone without fear of penalty or public condemnation. In the face of strong public opinion, no one would undertake to defend a witch or try to avenge such a person's death. Formal trials for witchcraft were rare, but from time to time, especially when fears were aroused by widespread sickness, Huron were slain as witches. When prominent chiefs became ill or died, their relatives frequently attributed their misfortune to witchcraft practiced by an enemy chief and demanded that a military raid be launched against the offending group. Thus, belief in witchcraft was a major factor sustaining intergroup warfare.

No one admitted to being a witch. The Huron believed, however, that clues to their identity could be found either in sick people's dreams or in the deviant behavior of the witches themselves. Overtly antisocial activities, such as a refusal to give feasts or to be sufficiently generous with neighbors, might arouse suspicion. Likewise, chronic secretiveness, aggressiveness, or any other form of unusual behavior constituted possible evidence of witchcraft. For the most part, these suspicions did not result in more than threats and veiled accusations meant to frighten individual men and women and induce them to conform with social norms. These pressures, together with the fear of angering witches, were a potent force discouraging idiosyncratic behavior and compelling all Huron to try to live according to the ideals of their society.

Unless subject to some form of social control, the right to slay suspected witches could have been used as an excuse for indiscriminate killings. The questions arise: Under what conditions could a Huron man (for it seems that only men slew witches) be certain that his society would recognize that the person he killed was a witch, and also under what circumstances were the murdered person's kin induced to accept this verdict and refrain from demanding compensation for the killing?

In many of the cases that are described in detail, the witches appear to have been slain on the orders of a village council or an individual chief. Chiefs are reported threatening men and women whose behavior had elicited their disapproval that they would accuse them of witchcraft and see they were killed unless they changed their ways. The threat of death was even formalized: "We will tear you out of the ground as a poisonous root." At least some accusations of witchcraft were discussed at secret council meetings of chiefs. Sometimes it appears that when a person was judged guilty, the verdict was pronounced *in absentia* and an executioner appointed to kill the witch without warning. These executions were carried out under the direction of the war chiefs, whose duty was to fight the enemies of Huron society. Most, if not all of the apparently spontaneous killings of witches were of this type.

In other instances the witch was arraigned for trial. It was once suggested to the Jesuits at a council meeting that a confession of witchcraft ought to be tortured out of them. In another case, a Huron woman was ostensibly invited to a feast. On arrival, she was accused of witchcraft and one of the war chiefs said that she ought to be killed immediately. Then she was tortured to make her reveal the names of any accomplices and told to name someone to be her executioner. She was further tortured with fire outside the house and finally her head was split open and her body burned. In this case, the parallel between the public execution of a witch and that of an enemy prisoner was quite explicit.

The association between chiefly sanction and the actual slaying of men and women as witches was an important control mechanism. No doubt, in spite of the rule that anyone could slay a witch, most people were restrained from killing even those they believed they had caught in the act by the fear that they would be accused of having murdered an innocent person. However, as long as chiefs could agree among themselves and mobilize public support, they were able to authorize such killings and use their power to do so to frighten individuals into seeking safety in socially approved forms of behavior.

The Jesuits also report that many murders committed by Huron were made to look like the work of Iroquois raiders. Sometimes this was done by individuals, but the chances of the deception being discovered seem to have been considerable. Yet, since chiefs investigated all cases of violent death to determine their causes, they had it in their power to declare that murders they did not choose to investigate further had in fact been committed by the enemy. A chief who held a high office in a ritual healing society threatened to kill one of its members and make it appear to be the work of the Iroquois after this woman had converted to Christianity. According to Huron beliefs, the woman had revealed herself to be a witch by refusing to continue to participate in the rituals of the healing society. Such behavior constituted indisputable evidence of her lack of concern for the welfare of others, which for the Huron was the essence of witchcraft.

The Huron did not clearly distinguish between witchcraft and serving the interests of enemy or rival groups. Traitors are said to have been killed in such a way that their deaths appeared to be the work of enemy raiders. The circumstantial evidence that surrounds the death of Joseph Chihwatenha, a convert who led the Jesuits into trading territory where the Huron did not wish them to go, suggests that he was killed on the orders of the Huron chiefs, although his death was attributed to the Iroquois. He also appears to have been thought guilty of witchcraft because of his close association with the Jesuits during the main period of epidemics. So serious had been his offenses that none of his relatives dared protest publicly about what had happened, although his brother, who had been until that time a fervent traditionalist, expressed a silent protest by converting to Christianity and adopting his brother's Christian name soon afterward.

Since the chiefs established the legitimacy of all killings of suspected witches and traitors, or dismissed them as the work of the enemy, they were in a position to eliminate particularly troublesome individuals and chronic offenders. This gave them additional power to coerce individuals whose behavior tended to be socially disruptive. Yet, for the use of such coercive power to be effective, the chiefs in any one community had to be certain that none of their number would publicly protest against what they had done. Most importantly, this meant securing the consent of the chiefs who belonged to the same clan segment as their intended victim. Since clan segments were bound to protect their members, agreement was only possible when the accused person's own family acknowledged that he or she was a witch. This could happen when public opinion was so aroused against an individual that relatives became frightened that they too would be accused of witchcraft if they continued to protect the accused, and there was no possibility of resolving the crisis by that person's household moving to another community. In most cases, these relatives would have pressured the victim to behave normally long before such a crisis arose. Making the killing of alleged witches appear to be the work of foreign raiders was a concession intended to lessen the public disgrace suffered by a clan segment that consented to the execution of one of its members. Yet, since everyone knew what had happened, these killings were no less efficacious in encouraging people to behave normally than were the rarer public executions of suspected witches.

At first glance, the fear of witchcraft would appear to have been a socially disruptive force. Yet the Huron chiefs were able to use crimes considered so heinous as to wipe out all considerations of kinship as a means for bringing pressure to bear upon individuals to behave in a socially responsible manner.

By making the individual Huron highly conscious of his or her neighbor's potential envy, witchcraft was also a strong force promoting a sense of community responsibility and assuring the realization of the communal and egalitarian ideals of Huron society. While ultimately based, like all other expressions of Huron authority, upon public opinion, the fear of witchcraft rationalized a form of coerciveness that was needed for the management of Huron society, but that the emphasis on individual dignity and the rights of Huron kin groups and clan segments made ideologically unacceptable.

8/Rituals and Celebrations

The Huron term *ondecha* meant the foundation, prop, or maintenance of a nation. It was used to refer to the dances, customs, and ceremonies that bound a people together and promoted friendship, solidarity, and goodwill among individuals regardless of their clan or lineage affiliations. Most of these activities had religious significance for the Huron. Like the other peoples of the northeastern woodlands, the Huron lacked specialists who performed regular religious ceremonies on behalf of the whole community. They did not construct special buildings, shrines, or altars for religious purposes, nor did they have a carefully defined religious creed. While the Huron shared a general set of religious beliefs, their religious behavior was open to innovation and borrowing from neighboring groups. Subject to the broad constraints of public opinion, each person was free to interpret and practice Huron religion as he or she wished. Yet, while religion did not have a carefully circumscribed sphere of its own in Huron life, this does not signify that it was unimportant to them. On the contrary, it tended to pervade all of their activities.

BELIEFS

Collective activities in Huron society were based upon shared beliefs. Like the activities, these beliefs cut across clan and national boundaries. They also served to bridge as well as to emphasize the gap between the male and female spheres of Huron life. Specialized knowledge of Huron religious beliefs and traditions was the property of a few elderly men and was transmitted from one generation of experts to another. At major feasts, when large numbers of people had gathered, these experts were called upon to recite their stories, which had as their central focus the creation of humanity and what had happened to the Huron since that time. In this way, a general knowledge of the traditions of the past was made known to the younger generation, and the solidarity of Huron society, past and present, was reaffirmed. That older men should guard and publicly transmit this knowledge was in keeping with the role that the elderly played in all aspects of Huron life. It is regrettable that so little of their lore was recorded in the seventeenth century.

The Huron lived in a world in which everything that existed, including objects that were made by human beings, had souls. Each individual had two sorts of souls. The first were life souls (*onnhekwi*), which animated the body and made each part of it function. These souls were as large and had the

106

same shape as the body, or organ, with which they were associated. They accounted for actions such as breathing, heartbeat, and bodily motion. Each of these manifestations of the body soul had its own name. The heart (*eiachia*) was associated with the emotions, especially courage and anger, which were the primary characteristics associated with warriors. It was for this reason that young men believed that they could acquire more courage by eating slices of the hearts of enemy warriors who had died bravely, in the same way that the human body sustained itself by ingesting, on a daily basis, the life forces that resided in corn, beans, fish, and mammals. An important characteristic of life souls was their inseparableness from the body.

The second sort of soul was the intellectual soul (*andionra*), which was associated with self-awareness, knowledge, memory, and the powers of reasoning. These were the qualities especially esteemed in civil chiefs. Intellect souls could travel in thoughts, dreams, and visions far beyond the body. For the Huron, thinking or dreaming about something was not an event that occurred within the mind of an individual; instead it involved the intellect soul traveling away from the body to visit the people or things that were the objects of its attention. This soul was also capable of communicating with the supernatural powers or spirits (*oki*) that animated the universe and possessed powers to do things that ordinary human beings could not do. These powers could be harnessed by human beings for good or evil purposes. Persons who had unusual powers or characteristics, such as shamans and witches, valiant warriors, unusually successful traders, and lunatics, were believed to possess companion spirits that endowed them with their special qualities. Because of this power, they too were considered to be *oki*. Charms, which by definition were the repositories of supernatural powers, were also called *oki*.

The spirits who resided in the earth, sky, rivers, lakes, and elsewhere in nature exerted control over trade, travel, war, diseases, human fertility, and every other aspect of human life. The most important of these spirits was the sky. It controlled the seasons, held in check the winds and waves, and assisted human beings in times of need. The sky was invoked whenever an important bargain or treaty was concluded, and it was believed that, if such an oath was broken, the sky would be certain to find and punish the offender. Offerings of tobacco were made to the sky, and it was thought highly improper and dangerous to mock it.

Like neighboring Algonkian peoples, the Huron believed that thunder was produced by a large bird that lived in the sky world. When he came to earth to feed, the flapping of his wings created a loud noise. In addition to controlling the rain, the thunderbird controlled insects, which multiplied in the dry season and threatened the Hurons' crops. Hence appeasing, or in some cases frightening away, the thunderbird was a matter of great concern to the Huron.

Certain large rocks were thought to be the homes of powerful spirits. Some were located along the trade routes that were frequented by the Huron. As travelers passed by these rocks, they made offerings to them. This was done by throwing tobacco into a campfire or placing it in clefts in the rock.

As they did so, the Huron would pray to the spirit of the rock to protect their homes and make their journey prosper. Even the familiar landscape of the Huron country abounded with the supernatural. One evil spirit, Atenchia-tennion ("he who changes and disguises himself"), was associated with Tan-dehwaronnon, a small hill near the community of Onnentisati in the Penetanguishene Peninsula. Another spirit, which resembled fire and lived on a large island near the Huron country, caused storms and fed on the corpses of those who had drowned.

Some supernatural beings appeared in human form in dreams and visions. Ondoutaehte, a spirit associated with warriors and perhaps a form of Ious-keha, manifested itself either as a male dwarf or as a woman. The most extensive data that have been preserved concern two of the most important and best personified Huron supernatural beings: Iouskeha and Aataentsik.

Iouskeha, the grandson of Aataentsik, had charge of the living. It was he who had made the world a suitable place for human beings. He created the lakes and rivers by freeing the waters that hitherto had been confined under the armpit of a supernatural frog. He also had released the animals from a great cave in which they had been concealed and had maimed each species in one leg so that they could be hunted more easily. The exception to this was the wolf, which he missed, and which remains hard to catch to this day. Iouskeha also made the corn grow and provided good weather. He had learned the secret of making fire from the great turtle, who was his ancestor, and had passed this knowledge on to human beings. As a patron spirit of warfare and prisoner sacrifice, he also maintained the vital forces of the natural cycle on which human beings depended. Iouskeha grew old as humans did, but never died since he was able to rejuvenate himself in old age and become a man in the prime of life.

Aataentsik was the first woman to appear on earth and the mother of all human beings. Her most direct matrilineal descendant was said to live among the Neutral. As a supernatural spirit, Aataentsik spent her time trying to undo the good works that Iouskeha had done. It was she who made human beings die. Aataentsik spread epidemics among the Huron and their neighbors and had charge of the souls of the dead. She was normally an old woman, but when she revealed herself to human beings, had the power to turn herself into a beautiful and fashionably dressed young girl. Iouskeha and Aataentsik were identified with the sun and moon, respectively.

These two supernatural beings were believed to live very much as the Huron did. Aataentsik even became ill occasionally and required the spirits of the dead to perform healing ceremonies for her. Iouskeha and Aataentsik had a longhouse far from the Huron country, which was surrounded by fields where they grew corn. Sometimes their dwelling was associated with the villages of the dead, which were believed to be located west of the Huron country. Occasionally, Huron traveling far from home came across this house. Aataentsik was likely to try to kill the visitors, although Iouskeha would attempt to save them. Iouskeha sometimes visited the Huron country. If he appeared in the cornfields carrying a well-developed stalk of corn, it signified a good harvest; if he were seen gnawing on a human leg, the crops would be bad. He also appeared to Huron in dreams in order to reveal what ceremonies they should perform to halt an epidemic, and would reveal himself to a number of individuals in the forest in the form of a giant carrying fish and ears of corn in order to reassure them in times of crisis. Iouskeha and Aataentsik also attended Huron festivals disguised as mortals. Iouskeha sometimes used these occasions to play tricks on Aataentsik.

Both of these supernatural beings played an important role in the Huron creation myth. The Huron believed that the world was a large island supported on the back of a turtle which swam in the primeval ocean. They also believed that the earth had a hole or burrow in it into which the sun set, coming out the other end the following morning. According to one account, an eclipse of the sun occurred when the turtle shifted his position and brought his shell in front of the sun.

The Huron believed that Aataentsik originally had dwelt in the sky. There the spirits live much as people do on earth. One day, either when chasing a bear or cutting down a tree to make medicine for her husband, Aataentsik dropped through a hole in the sky and began to fall earthwards. The great turtle saw her fall and asked the other aquatic animal spirits swimming in the primeval sea to dive to the bottom and bring up soil, which they were to pile on his back. In this way the earth was formed and Aataentsik landed gently on it.

When Aataentsik fell, she was pregnant. Eventually she became the maternal grandmother of two boys: Iouskeha and Atawiskaron. Iouskeha was born in the normal fashion, but Atawiskaron aggressively cut his way out of his mother's womb, killing her in the process. Atawiskaron had inherited many of Aataentsik's malevolent qualities and spent much of his time trying to undo the good works his brother had performed for human beings. Eventually the two brothers engaged in mutual combat. Atawiskaron fought with the fruits of a wild rosebush and Iouskeha with the horns of a stag. Iouskeha struck his brother so hard that the blood flowed. As he fled, the drops of his blood fell on the ground and were turned into flint (*atawiskara*), which the Indians later used to make stone tools and weapons.

These myths provide a fascinating commentary on Huron social organization. The idea that Aataentsik was the female ancestor of the human race and the unimportance they attach to paternity, as opposed to mother-son relationships, are straightforward reflections of the matrilineal bias of Huron society. Another untransformed aspect of these stories is their recognition that, while Huron men and women lived very different lives, they ultimately depended upon one another and had to live together. Yet the roles assigned to Iouskeha and Aataentsik are in many ways the direct opposite of those played by men and women in everyday life. Among the Huron, men committed most of the real and symbolic acts of violence. It was they who cut down the forests, killed fish and animals, and hunted one another. Women were associated with life-producing and life-sustaining activities. They bore children, grew crops, and cared for the home. Iouskeha is portrayed as having made the world habitable and filling it with plants and animals that are useful to human beings. He made crops grow and protected human beings from all kinds of malevolent influences. While he was capable of violence (he fought and wounded his twin brother), he was primarily associated with benevolent and creative endeavors. Far from helping to sustain life, Aataentsik sought to spoil the good Iouskeha had accomplished. She afflicted human beings with death and sought to hurt them whenever she could.

It is possible that by conferring important human gender characteristics on mythological figures of the opposite sex, these stories attempted to compensate both sexes for the limitations that were inherent in the roles assigned to them in real life. Women, on the one hand, were mythologically endowed with dangerous and aggressive qualities. They may have possessed some of these characteristics in the imaginations of adult males, who felt threatened by the demands of their wives' relatives and were rarely more than guests in their wives', or even their mothers', longhouses. Yet these qualities were far removed from the hard work and undramatic nature of the lives women normally experienced in their settlements and cornfields. Women may have envied men their freedom and adventures in the forest, but at the same time felt relieved that they did not have to expose themselves to the many dangers that men did. On the other hand, in the creation legend, men had their principal role as destroyers of life complemented by a symbolic role as its sustainers. This reinforced, in a less demanding fashion, the other symbolic life-supporting role that they were believed to play, by shedding their own and each other's blood in warfare and torture rituals in order to sustain the life force of the universe. However much Huron men may have glorified in being self-reliant warriors, they remained to a large extent materially and psychologically dependent on their female relatives. Hence it may have gratified them to imagine their chief male spirit as a creator and sustainer of life and the primeval female spirit as its destroyer. The ambivalence that men felt about their role may have been further symbolized by Iouskeha's attack upon his brother, who seems to have shared Aataentsik's destructive and aggressive nature. It is surely no accident that Atawiskaron's blood turned to flint, the stone that was used to make weapons.

FEASTS

The Huron enjoyed giving and attending feasts. Generosity was an important means of winning the respect and approval of others. For this reason, families worked hard to grow the corn, obtain the meat, and accumulate the presents necessary to entertain and oblige their friends and neighbors. The desire to excel at this was probably the main incentive for hard work among the Huron.

Each of the Huron peoples had its own dances and ceremonies. When refugees, such as the Wenro, came to live among the Huron, they brought still more customs with them. Once these had been introduced, they spread from one Huron community to another. For this reason, it is impossible to treat descriptions of Huron customs as representing either a static pattern or one that was common to all four Huron peoples.

According to the Jesuits, the Huron had four types of feasts. The largest and most important were the *atonronta aochien*, or singing feasts. Often hundreds of guests from all over the Huron country attended these feasts, and many kettles of food containing deer and large fish, as well as bear and dog meat, were prepared. Singing feasts were given if a man wished to become renowned, which usually meant at the investitures of new chiefs, or before launching a major military campaign. Feasts of this type were also part of the celebrations that accompanied the annual meeting of the confederacy council.

The second type was the *enditenhwa*, or thanksgiving feast. These were less elaborate than the singing feasts and appear to have been given by individuals to celebrate their personal good fortune. If a man had been particularly successful at fishing, hunting, or trading, he gave a feast for his friends or, if he could afford it, for the whole village upon his return home. Individuals who had escaped from danger or recovered from a serious illness likewise sponsored a feast to celebrate their good fortune. From time to time, the owner of a charm gave a feast to restore or increase its power, by honoring and nurturing the spirit that empowered it. All of these feasts were probably classified as *enditenhwa*.

The final two categories of feasts were curing feasts and *atsataion* or farewell feasts. The latter were given by people on the point of dying. Both of these will be described in Chapter 10.

When a group decided to sponsor a feast, its chief sent out invitations well in advance. He or his specially appointed messengers went about contacting the guests. Sometimes he issued a public announcement requesting the whole community to attend. Special invitations were sent to chiefs in neighboring communities, and sometimes bundles of sticks were carried to each settlement representing the number of other people who were invited. The sticks were distributed by the local chiefs among the inhabitants of each settlement. It was regarded as an insult for anyone who was personally invited to a feast not to come, unless that person had a good reason for not doing so.

People who were invited to a feast arrived wearing their finest clothing and ornaments. Their hair was carefully made up and their faces and bodies were often painted (Fig.20). Each guest brought his or her own plate and spoon. Singing and dancing sometimes began before the meal was served, sometimes afterward. Most, and perhaps all, of the eating and dancing took place indoors. Inside the longhouse where the feast was to be held, the guests sat on mats and cedar boughs that were spread on the ground and on top of the platforms along either side. The men seated themselves towards the upper end of the longhouse, the women at the lower, as Iroquois still do today in their traditional religious observances. Only those who were invited to the feast entered the longhouse, and once the guests had arrived the doors were

Figure 20. Huron girl dressed for dance. From Champlain's Voyages *of 1619.*

closed. After this, no one was supposed to enter the house. Failure to observe this rule was believed to bring bad luck and to affect adversely the purpose for which the feast was being given.

The singing at feasts was led by two chiefs who stood in the midst of the dancers, each holding a turtle-shell rattle in his hand. The dancers formed an oval around these chiefs. The chiefs sang the refrains; the dancers replied: "Hé, Hé, Hé," and shouted loudly at the end of each song. The dancers did not hold hands, but kept their fists clenched. The women placed their fists on top of each other and held their arms straight out from their bodies; men waved their arms as if they were brandishing weapons. The dancers stamped their feet on the ground, one at a time and in tune with the song. The women shook their whole bodies and, after four or five steps, the dancers turned toward the person next to them and inclined their heads. Dances were expected to be performed vigorously and to be accompanied by appropriate facial gestures (Figs.21,22).

If the feast lasted all day, and some lasted for several days, food was served both in the morning and in the afternoon. When a meal was ready, messengers went through the community or mounted the roof of the longhouse to summon the guests. Once they had all assembled, the meal began in a formal fashion. The person giving the feast, or a deputy, announced *onne aokwira*, "the kettle has boiled." To express their approval, all the guests replied, "Ho," and struck the ground or sleeping platforms with their fists. Then the sponsor of the feast went through the longhouse announcing the

Figure 21. Huron dance. From Champlain's Voyages *of 1619. Unlike most dances described by seventeenth-century authors, this one is located out-of-doors. The pot in the foreground is a metal trade kettle.*

contents of each kettle *yanniennon iouri* "there is cooked dog," *oskennonton iouri*, "there is a deer cooked." The guests again replied, "Ho," and struck the ground with their fists. Then the servers went from row to row taking each person's bowl and filling it from the kettles. Some of the flesh of the larger animals was roasted, and pieces of it were passed around as well.

Guests invited to a feast were expected to eat heartily. At some of them they were required to consume everything in the kettles, even if they had to empty their stomachs by vomiting in order to do so. Alternatively, people who could not finish their portions might persuade friends to eat for them, often giving them a small present as a token of appreciation. These were called "eat all" feasts, and they usually had a ritual purpose. At feasts the spokesman or principal host ate little or nothing at all. He spent his time smoking, singing, and entertaining his guests. Strangers and visitors from other settlements were given the choicest food, and the heads of the animals

Figure 22. Another drawing of Iroquoian dancers. From Novae Franciae Accurata Delineatio.

cooked for feasts were presented as trophies to the most important chiefs who were in attendance.

Various dances and rites were considered appropriate to particular kinds of feasts. Often these activities were ascribed a supernatural origin, knowledge of them having been revealed by a spirit in the course of a dream or vision. In addition to eating and dancing, feasts were often enlivened by games and contests.

ONNONHWAROIA

The majority of Huron celebrations took place in the winter months or in the late autumn and early spring, when most people were staying in their settlements. During the summer the women were busy tending their crops and men often traveled far away from their communities fighting, trading, and fishing. There is no evidence that the Huron celebrated the calendrical festivals, such as Seed Planting, Corn Sprouting, Green Corn, and Harvest that in later times were such important features of Five Nations Iroquois ritual. Fenton (1940:164) has observed that these Iroquois ceremonies, which seem to be derived from the southeastern United States, are dominated by the idea of renewal and mark the annual crises in maize cultivation, although other calendrical rituals were associated with the harvesting of wild fruit, especially strawberries. Rituals that now form part of the Iroquois Midwinter ceremonies are reported in descriptions of Huron culture, but the context in which they appear seems to be entirely different. Tooker (1960:70–1) has suggested that since the seventeenth century, the principal emphasis in northern Iroquoian ceremonialism has shifted from shamanistic practices and curing ceremonies to calendrical rituals. The principal changes appear to have been brought about by the "new religion" of Handsome Lake, which began at the end of the eighteenth century (Wallace 1970).

The main Huron winter ceremony was the *onnonhwaroia* ("one's head is agitated" or "the upsetting of the brain"). While this festival appears to have been observed at least once a year in each community, it was not a calendrical observance. The reason given for performing it was either that many people in the community had become depressed or were physically ailing, or that some prominent man or woman was languishing and it was believed that the ceremony would help cure that person. The *onnonhwaroia* began in the evening with bands of people who felt depressed or threatened by sickness going through the settlement singing and shouting in a wild fashion. These people entered all of the houses, where they proceeded to upset furnishings, break pots, and toss firebrands about. Occasionally these activities resulted in a house catching on fire. The next day they returned and announced that each of them had dreamed about something. People were called upon to guess the nature of these dreams and to present each person with the object that his or her dream had revealed. As these people went from one family to another, they were given kettles, knives, pipes, live dogs, skins, fish, tobacco, and many other kinds of presents in the hope that one of them might be the object they were seeking. Hints concerning what they wanted were given in the form of riddles. One person would say, "What I want and see is that which bears a lake within itself," by which he meant that he was looking for a squash. Another might ask for "What I see in my eyes, it will be marked with various colors." This meant a glass trade bead, since in Huron the same word was used for "eye" and "glass bead." At each hearth the dreamers recited or displayed the objects that they had already been offered, in order to make it easier for the next person to guess their dreams. If someone refused to give a person a present, he or she went outside, picked up a stone, and placed it in front of that person as a sign of reproach. When dreamers were finally given what they were looking for, they interpreted it as a sign that the troubles that were threatening them had been averted. They thanked their benefactors, uttered a cry of joy, and rushed out of the house. Everyone else struck their hands on the ground and shouted "Hé,é,é,é,é!" to congratulate them. The *onnonhwaroia* usually lasted three days, at the end of which the participants went into the forest to cast out their madness. Afterward, they returned all the presents they had received except the ones they had dreamed about.

Special feasts might be held if a community felt threatened by disaster. One shaman prescribed a feast in order to avert the misfortune that was augured by a lunar eclipse that had taken place in an inauspicious location in the sky. Shamans also recommended feasts as a means of averting drought or dangerous frosts. During one epidemic, large masks were erected over the doors of houses, and archers fashioned out of straw were placed on the roofs of houses in order to frighten away the spirits that were causing people to die. In seeking to avert such threats, the Huron reaffirmed their own social identity.

CURING SOCIETIES

The Huron had numerous formal associations that cut across clan and community divisions. One such type of institution was the curing societies, each of which performed specific rituals that were believed to cure certain kinds of diseases. The Huron dreaded sickness and considered the activities of these societies to be very important. We have already noted that a woman was threatened with death when she refused to participate any longer in the activities of one of these societies as a result of her conversion to Christianity.

Each curing society had a leader, whose office was hereditary. Often these leaders were important chiefs whose ritual office complemented and strengthened their secular one. People whom the society had cured were invited to become members, and after their deaths their membership could be inherited matrilineally. Thus, the members of these societies were drawn from many different households and often from many communities. Various dances appear to have been the property of each of these curing societies.

One curing society was the *atirenda*. It consisted of about eighty people, including six women. This society was first reported in the eastern part of the confederacy and did not gain any members among the Attignawantan until 1636. Its principal dance was the *otakrendoiae*. In this dance the members of the society simulated killing each other using charms such as bears' claws, wolves' teeth, stones, and dog sinews. As the members fell under the spell of these charms, blood poured from their mouths and nostrils as they bit their cheeks or appeared to as the more timid used red ochre mixed with saliva as a substitute. The members of this society were reputed to be skilled in treating hernias, but they were also rumored to avenge insults by giving patients they did not like poison instead of medicine. One initiate was given a charm in the form of a little doll which he put in his tobacco pouch and which he claimed stirred inside it and began to order feasts and ceremonies be performed in its honor. Parallels have been noted between this society and the *midewiwin* ceremonies found among various Algonkian peoples of the Upper Great Lakes region (Tooker 1964:99).

Another society performed the curing dance known as the *ataenrohwi* ("hot cinders dance"), which is described as the most general remedy that the Huron had for sickness. The rituals of this society were extremely dramatic and impressive. Its members handled burning charcoal and stones that had been heated red hot. Some chewed hot charcoal, and after warming their hands by blowing on them rubbed the affected part of the patient's body. Others blew or spit pieces of charcoal on the sick person. Still others put live coals into their mouths and growled like bears into the patient's ear or danced holding red hot stones in their mouths. After short bursts of such frenzied activity, the members lay down and fell asleep, or all of them sweated for a time under blankets. During these dances so much burning material was scattered about the longhouse that its occupants removed everything of value for fear the longhouse might catch fire. Some members of the society found that they could not handle hot coals and only pretended to do so. One man, who admitted that he had done this, said that eventually he dreamed that he could handle fire and heard a song that he remembered when he awoke. He sang this song at the next dance the society performed and found that henceforth he could easily handle hot stones and plunge his arms into boiling kettles.

Masked dancers performed rituals to drive away sickness. In one such dance, the members appeared disguised as hunchbacks carrying sticks and wearing wooden masks. It has been suggested that this society was similar to the Iroquois False Faces (Blau 1966). In other curing rituals women walked on all fours, like animals. They may have belonged to groups similar to the Iroquois Bear and Buffalo societies, whose members imitate the animal after which the association is named. Other dancers wore sacks over their faces or stuffed straw around their waists so that they resembled pregnant women. Fenton has compared these two groups with the Iroquois Longnose and Husk Face Impersonators. Still other men attended curing feasts wearing bearskins that covered the whole body, with the ears on top of the head and the face covered. These acted as doorkeepers and took part in the dances only at intervals. If a dog were sacrificed, one of them would carry it in, throw it on the ground several times until it was dead, and give it to the person who would prepare it to be eaten at the end of the dance. A reference to a man who was the leader of the "Dance of the Naked Ones" probably records the name of yet another curing society. The members of these groups were rewarded for their efforts with a feast and presents from the sick man and his relatives.

FRIENDSHIP

Ritual friendships were a formal, lifelong relationship between two people of the same sex that entailed specific mutual rights and obligations. Lalemant describes a woman being commanded in a dream to become the friend of another woman. To accomplish this, she gave the woman a dog, a blanket, and a load of firewood and finally invited her and her husband to a feast that was intended to formalize the friendship.

A less formal social activity that brought men together was the sweat bath. Sweating was done either for purely social or for religious reasons. The *arontontawan* or *atiatarihati* was a sweat lodge constructed for social reasons, while the *endeon* was a ceremonial sweat lodge. In the latter, a sick man or a shaman would seek a curing vision. Quite apart from its religious role, any sweat lodge was thought to promote health by cleansing the body (Steckley 1989).

When a man wished to sweat, he invited his friends to join him. The sweating was done inside a small, circular hut that was heated by placing hot stones in the center. Because sweathouses were easy to construct, they were used not only in settlements but also in overnight camps while traveling. Especially in the winter, they were erected inside longhouses. The men huddled closely together inside the hut, their knees raised against their stomachs.

Then someone outside covered the hut with skins and pieces of bark so that no heat could escape. To encourage sweating, one of the men inside the hut sang, while the rest shouted continuously as they did in their dances. They also drank large potfuls of cold water and sometimes burned tobacco. When the sweating was over, they closed their pores by jumping into a nearby river or washing in cold water.

GAMES

Games were an extremely important means of promoting social interaction, especially between men from neighboring settlements. Sometimes games were played among individuals from the same community, but not infrequently teams from different communities competed with one another. These games generated great interest and provided people from these settlements with an opportunity to engage in friendly rivalry and enjoy each other's company. The Huron were avid gamblers, and no game, however informal, was unaccompanied by a wager. Luck in gambling was thought to testify to the supernatural powers that were at a person's disposal. Hence games provided another opportunity for the redistribution of material possessions among the Huron. The stakes often ran high. One village lost thirty wampum belts in a single match, and some individuals gambled away even the clothes they wore. One person, having lost all he owned, staked his hair, and when he lost again cut it off without any sign of regret. Another man gambled his little finger and on losing cut it off. The Jesuits stated that gambling was a frequent cause of fights and murders, but this seems to be an error. Elsewhere they noted that men and women who had gambled away everything returned home as cheerful as if they had lost nothing. Such public conduct was in keeping with the spirit of Huron culture and with Huron attitudes towards property. Yet some individuals were sufficiently ashamed of their losses that they committed suicide rather than return home to face their families. This reflects the personal humiliation that Huron felt about actions which squandered the wealth of their kin group in situations that did not result in anyone gaining social prestige. The imprudent gambler was shamed by precisely the same considerations that shamed a murderer.

The three games that the Huron played most commonly were lacrosse, the dish game, and *aheskara*. These games were familiar to most of the peoples living around the Great Lakes and had religious significance in all their cultures. They were often played to cure the sick or to prevent disaster. Lacrosse matches are reported to have been held to avert public misfortune, stop an epidemic, influence the weather, and honor the memory of a dead player.

Lacrosse was played with a ball and sticks in a field outside the village. It was a dangerous game involving mostly young men, who were frequently injured. Like warfare, it served as a test of personal bravery. The dish game was played with five or six fruit stones or small pottery disks painted black on one side and yellow or white on the other. In an ordinary game the players seated themselves in a circle and each one in turn placed the stones in a wooden bowl and then struck it sharply on the ground. One side scored when all the stones fell out with either one color or the other facing up. Women sometimes played with the stones, but they did not use the bowl. They took the stones in their hands and threw them into the air, letting them fall on a skin or hide stretched on the ground. Occasionally, men and boys played this game with the women. Even in these family games, however, collars, earrings, and other possessions were wagered. The third game, *aheskara*, was played with three hundred or four hundred white rushes, each about a foot long. The rules governing this game are unknown, but it may have involved a player grabbing a specific number of reeds or guessing how many an opponent held.

In one instance, a prominent individual asked the chiefs of his settlement to have the dish game played for his health. The chiefs agreed and held a council to fix the time of the game and decide what community should be challenged to play. When the challenge was accepted, preparations for the game began in both settlements. The men who were to be on each team fasted and abstained from sexual intercourse, as they did on any occasion when they sought supernatural powers. Then they assembled at night for a feast, during which they performed sleight-of-hand tricks intended to win them the favor of the playing stones and resorted to divination to predict the outcome of the match. They also brought out their personal charms and exhorted them to bring them good luck. After this, they slept in hopes of having a favorable dream or one in which still further charms would be revealed.

In the morning they revealed their dreams and collected all the items they believed would bring them good luck. On the day of the game, the teams and spectators from the two communities arranged themselves on opposite sides of a large longhouse, completely filling it. The sick man, for whom the game was being played, was brought in, and the two players who were to start took their positions in the middle of the longhouse. When the bets between individuals on both sides had been arranged, the game began. All of the spectators shouted and gestured in an effort either to attract luck for their player or to drive misfortune to the other side of the house. Each side had a man who kept track of points lost and won. A player who was unlucky was soon replaced by another member of his team. Such a game might continue for several days, with food and hospitality being provided for everyone who attended.

Feasts, dances, and games were, as the Huron said, the prop of their society. These activities crosscut lineages and clan segments and brought together the inhabitants of different communities in celebrations and friendly rivalry. In the next chapter the most solemn and far reaching of all the Huron efforts for promoting social solidarity, the Feast of the Dead, will be examined.

9/The Dead

The Huron were grateful for their earthly existence and did not believe that life after death would be an improvement. On the contrary, death seemed to threaten a diminishment and dispersal of the life forces that animated human beings. They also believed that what happened to them after death was determined not by how they had behaved during their lifetime but by their physical condition when they died and what had caused their death. It was further influenced by what happened to their souls in a transitional period lasting a decade or more following death. In many different ways death threatened to disrupt the social relations on which every individual's happiness depended.

Given these views, it is not surprising that the Huron, like most North American Indians, did not practice any sort of ancestor worship; nor did they look to the dead for favors and support (Tooker 1968:14). On the contrary, they tended to fear the souls of the dead because they believed that most of them resented not being able to behave as they had done while alive. Although the Huron greatly mourned and cherished the memory of recently deceased relatives and friends, their long-term goal was to create a barrier that would separate the worlds of the living and the dead. This ambivalent attitude towards the dead may help to explain why the most impressive Huron ceremonies were associated with burial, and also why it took a decade or longer to complete the burial rituals associated with any one individual.

In addition to trying to separate the living and the dead, the Huron minimized the impact of death in many aspects of their everyday life. This was done through the inheritance of names, as a result of which chiefs appeared to live from one generation to another. A Huron visiting a community after an interval of forty or fifty years would know the names of the various chiefs of that community and what specific duties each of them had. Once a captive was adopted to replace a dead Huron, he not only was given the name of that person but was eligible to inherit the same offices.

Death was a source of great anxiety to the Huron. This was true partly because it was viewed as cutting off effective personal contact between the living and individuals they loved. It was a grievous injury to remind a person of any relative who had died, especially one who had done so recently. Merely to say "your dead relatives" was a curse capable of bringing people to blows. To mention someone's name without adding an honorific to indicate that

120

person was dead was a serious insult. This was one of the reasons why chiefs quickly announced a person's death throughout the community. If anyone living there had the same name as the dead person, he or she changed it for a time in order not to offend the relatives of the deceased. Great respect was also shown for the remains of the dead. If fire broke out in a community, greater efforts were directed to saving the cemetery than saving the houses.

In their concern for mortuary rituals, the Huron were the heirs of a longstanding tradition among the native peoples of eastern North America. Yet the periodic reburial of the dead in large bone pits or ossuaries, which was of such great importance to them, was a custom not shared by the Iroquois of New York State. This practice was foreshadowed in the interment of bundles containing the disarticulated bones of one or more individuals in and around settlements in the region north of Lake Ontario during early Iroquoian times (Wright 1966:99). In the fourteenth century, small ossuaries began to be constructed close to Huron settlements. Later, the ossuaries grew larger as settlements increased in size and bigger political groupings began to play a more important role in Huron life. By the historic period, the Feast of the Dead, of which ossuary burial was the principal feature, had become the most important of all rituals for binding together the different Huron peoples and cementing relations between the Huron and their northern trading partners.

BELIEFS ABOUT THE DEAD

The powers of an individual that survived after death were called *asken*, which was yet another word meaning soul (Steckley 1978). When the corpse was carried to the cemetery, its soul was believed to walk ahead of it and to remain near the body until the Feast of the Dead. At night the souls of those who were buried in the community cemetery wandered through the settlement, entering houses and eating what was left of the evening meal. Some Huron would not eat food that had been left standing overnight for fear they would die if they consumed what belonged to the dead.

The Huron believed that the dead, like the living, had two souls. One sort, which shared many features with the life soul of a living person, remained with the body after the Feast of the Dead until it was reborn in a child. According to the Huron, such reincarnations explained why children often resembled their dead ancestors. Because of the Huron belief in this soul, the bones of the dead were called *atisken*, "the souls." The other soul, which had more in common with the intellect soul, left the body at the Feast of the Dead and traveled to a village of the dead located near the western edge of the world. Each Huron people or large community was believed to have its counterpart in the land of the dead, where Aataentsik and Iouskeha also lived. These souls were thought to fly westward in the form of flocks of passenger pigeons or to move along the Milky Way, which was called *atisken ondahate*, "the path of souls." Certain stars near the Milky Way, which were called *yanniennon ondahate*, "the path of dogs," were the route by which the souls of these domestic animals traveled westward. On still other occasions, the route to the west was identified with the trail leading from the Huron to the Tionontati country. It passed a large standing rock called Ekarenniondi, which was said to be daubed with the paint spirits used on their faces. Farther along this road, the souls came across the house of the spirit Oskotarach, "Pierce-Head." He drew the brains out of the heads of the dead and kept them in pumpkins. This act may have removed from souls the memory of their former life, or at least the desire to return to the world of the living (Steckley 1978). Still farther west there was a deep river that had to be crossed on a bridge made of a fallen tree trunk. This bridge was guarded by a fierce dog that made many souls fall into the river and drown.

In the villages of the dead, life was in many respects the same as it had been among the living. The souls tilled the soul, went hunting and fishing, and participated in feasts and dances. The inhabitants of this realm became sick from time to time but could be cured by these ceremonies. The souls of food and utensils that the living had buried with the dead were used by them in the afterlife. Yet in spite of these similarities to the land of the living, the souls of the dead were said to have complained day and night, although from time to time their chiefs tried to make them stop. Among the major differences between the world of the dead and that of the living, there is no evidence that souls ever gave birth to children.

Not every mobile soul joined the conventional villages of the dead. Because they lacked strength for the journey, the souls of old people and children remained in the Huron country, where they had their own villages. They sowed corn in the fields that the living had abandoned, and if a village caught fire, collected the burned corn for their own use. These souls were heard by the living from time to time, but because they were weak, they were not regarded as dangerous. The bodies of fetuses or babies only a few months old were buried under paths so that their souls might enter the womb of a woman who was passing by and be reborn (Steckley 1986b). The Huron believed that the souls of people who had died violent deaths, including suicides, were dangerous, and for that reason were excluded from the regular villages of the dead. The souls of those who died in battle formed a band of their own, one that was feared by other Huron souls.

The bodies of those who had died violent deaths were immediately buried or burned, and were not dug up and reburied at the Feast of the Dead. The bones of captives who were tortured found their way into the village middens, and the corpses of some who were slain on charges of witchcraft were publicly burned. The body of a person who had drowned or froze to death was taken to a community cemetery and laid on a mat. A grave was dug on one side of the body and a fire lighted on the other. Then some young men, chosen by the relatives of the deceased, cut up the body and threw the flesh and entrails into the fire, while the skeleton was buried in the grave. This ritual was performed to appease the spirit of the sky or of a lake, who was believed to be angry. Failure to do this would have resulted in dangerous changes in the weather and in accidents. Thus the men who cut up the body were rewarded for having performed a public-spirited act. If a Huron died far from home, his body was burned and the bones extracted to be carried back to his home town.

The Huron claimed knowledge of the hereafter from souls that had visited them in dreams and from visits that the living had made to the land of the dead. One Huron story told of a man who, after many adventures, brought the soul of his sister (not his wife) back from the realm of the dead, having struggled with it all night in order to make it small enough to fit into a pumpkin. Oskotarach had told him that he could restore her to life by sponsoring a feast, in the course of which the brains Oskotarach had removed and kept in another pumpkin could be recombined with her body; however, Oskotarach warned that no one who was present could watch what was happening. When the man returned home, he made a feast as Oskotarach had counseled, but as he was attempting to resuscitate his sister, some inquisitive guest raised his eyes and her soul escaped.

DEATH AND BURIAL OF INDIVIDUALS

A Huron was expected to die as well as to live bravely. Dying persons often inspected the clothing in which they were to be buried and frequently were dressed for burial before they died. They also gave an *atsataion*, or farewell feast, for their friends and relatives during which, if they were able, they partook of the best food, and a man would sing his war song to show that he did not fear death. These feasts were also given in honor of prisoners who were about to be tortured. Members of the community vied with each other to present dying people with anything they requested, believing that satisfying their desires might cause them to recover. Death was frequently attributed to failure to provide for the wishes of a person's soul; hence, someone who refused to give a dying person what he or she wanted might be held responsible for that person's death and even accused of witchcraft by the deceased's relatives. On the other hand, if an individual who was believed to be about to die recovered, the last present that had been given was credited with saving that person's life and treasured as long as he or she lived. The sick person and his or her relatives were also morally indebted to whomever had given the present, as well as to that person's family.

As soon as people died, their bodies were flexed in a crouching position, wrapped tightly in their finest fur robe, and laid on the mat on which they had died. Among some of the Huron peoples, the friends and relatives of the deceased painted their faces black and also painted the face of the dead person and embellished his or her body with feathers and other ornaments. Every family had people who were specially appointed to take charge of their dead. It is likely that particular families belonging to different clans, and opposite moieties, were responsible for attending to the details of each other's funerals. This not only created another strong bond of reciprocity within Huron society but also freed the relatives of the deceased from having to worry about funeral arrangements during their period of deepest mourning.

As soon as he was informed that someone had died, a chief or his assistant went through the settlement announcing who had died and urging each family to prepare some food and distribute it among the friends and relatives of the deceased. When the food was ready, the people of the community converged on the longhouse of the dead person for a wake-like observance called the *ayochien atisken*, "feast of souls." During this observance, the women and girls of the community wept in a highly stylized manner, making their voices tremble in one accord. Each woman inflamed her grief by reciting the names of all her relatives who had died. This wailing and grief continued until a chief ordered them to stop. During this time the men did not weep, but assumed a melancholy expression, with their heads sunk on their knees. Frequently, someone spoke to comfort the relatives of the deceased, pointing out the inevitability of death and praising the dead person's personality, good nature, generosity, and bravery.

Burial usually took place on the third day after death. This gave relatives and friends in far-off Huron communities time to arrive for the funeral. If the deceased had been a person of consequence, not only large numbers of friends but also important chiefs from other communities would assemble, each bearing presents in the dead person's honor. The funeral began at day-break with a meal. This was provided to feed the guests who had arrived from elsewhere, to nourish the soul of the dead person, and as a further expression of the grief and consolation of the community. When all the kettles were emptied, those attending the funeral assembled inside the house of the dead person and mourning resumed. The body was then covered with a beaver robe and four men carried it on a mat to the cemetery, the mourners following in silence. In the cemetery, a tomb had been prepared. Normally these consisted of a bark coffin painted with various designs and supported on posts about three meters high (Fig.23). In some communities a few corpses were buried in the ground, a bark hut was built over their grave, and a stake fence erected around it. These structures were probably erected over the graves of individuals who had died violent deaths.

When everyone had arrived at the cemetery, an official publicly announced the presents that had been given to dry the tears of the spouse and other relatives of the deceased. These presents were distributed among the relatives and those who had taken charge of the funeral. Only an occasional wampum belt, a comb, a gourd full of oil, or a few loaves of bread were placed in the coffin with the deceased. At some funerals, when the coffin was closed, two sticks were thrown from the top of the tomb to the young men and women who had gathered on either side. A fierce struggle ensued, the aim of which was for one person to gain possession of each stick and win a prize. When the burial was finished, everyone departed quickly for home.

For ten days after the funeral, the dead person's spouse lay, like the dead, on a mat, covered with furs, and with his or her face pressed against the ground. During this period, such mourners did not speak, except to say good-day to visitors. They did not warm themselves by the fire and only left the

Figure 23. A Huron cemetery. From Champlain's Voyages *of 1619. A normal scaffold burial and a specialized inhumation are depicted.*

house at night to go to the toilet. Widows did not comb their hair or clean themselves during this period.

This initial deep mourning was followed by a year when courtship and remarriage did not take place. During this period, widows and widowers did not grease their hair and avoided friends and going to feasts. Women observed greater extremes of mourning during this period than men did. They frequently blackened their faces and went about ill-clad, unkempt, and with their heads lowered (a sign of unsociability). They also frequently visited the cemetery to mourn. Sometimes, however, a widow's mother might persuade her to cease her grief and resume normal life before the year was ended.

Deaths also imposed restrictions on the friends of the deceased. Men usually did not go fishing for some time after a friend had died, as fish were believed to dislike the dead. Feasts were given in memory of the dead from time to time. The most important of these were connected with conferring the title of a dead chief upon his successor.

THE FEAST OF THE DEAD

The bodies of people who had not died violent deaths did not remain in the village cemeteries, but were removed from their coffins and reburied in a common bone pit at the Feast of the Dead, an observance that the Huron colloquially referred to as *yandatsa*, "the kettle." This ceremony was held approximately every ten or fifteen years.

The Feast of the Dead was planned by the chiefs of each Huron people, who sought to make it a national festival. Yet it appears to have been celebrated every time a large community changed location. The number of ossuaries in the Huron country that contain substantial trade goods, and thus probably date after 1580, indicates that the more populous Huron nations each must have celebrated more than one Feast of the Dead, if these ceremonies were observed at intervals of ten years or more. Furthermore, even the largest of these ossuaries contains the bones of only about 1000 individuals, which, assuming a normal death rate of 2.7 people per hundred each year (it would have been much higher during the epidemics of the 1630s), indicates that such an ossuary served a population of no more than 3000–4000 people. This is too small for a group as numerous as the Attignawantan and accords with the observation that they celebrated two Feasts of the Dead in 1636, one in the northern part of the country, another in the south. The best explanation appears to be that a Feast of the Dead was held each time that a large community changed location and that into its ossuary were placed the dead of that community and of smaller neighboring settlements. Once the community moved, there would have been no one to protect and care for its cemetery; hence, the interment of its dead was a way of ensuring their safety, while their bones remained close to the site where they had been born or died. The ritual, by marking a definitive break between the living and the dead, also conformed to Huron beliefs about what was necessary to ensure the eternal well-being of both.

All Huron communities were informed whenever a Feast of the Dead was to be held so that those who wished that particular ossuary to be the final burial place of their relatives might bring them there. Some of the bodies brought from a distance were those of natives of the settlement who had married and died elsewhere. Apparently the desire of friends to be buried together also caused people to request burial in an ossuary other than that of their own settlement. The significance of this mingling of the dead from many parts of the Huron country in the ossuary of a single community was very important to the Huron. They said that because the bones of their relatives and friends were united in the same place, they themselves felt obliged to live in unity and concord. Friendly peoples from outside the confederacy were also invited to the ceremony; thus, it tended to reinforce ties not only among the Huron but also between the Huron and their allies. It is unclear to what degree groups outside the confederacy were encouraged to bury the bodies of a few of their members in Huron ossuaries to reinforce their alliance. The Attignawantan sought permission from the Jesuits to exhume and rebury the bodies of two Frenchmen who had died in the Huron country. On the other hand, this same people boasted that the souls of Algonkian would not be welcomed in their villages of the dead. This suggests that they may not have permitted the bones of Algonkians to be mingled with their own.

The Feast of the Dead lasted ten days. The first eight were spent preparing the bodies for reburial and assembling the participants, some of whom had to come from a considerable distance. Some attended solely as spectators, others to bury their dead. In each community where there were the latter, people went to the cemeteries, and those who had charge of burying a particular body removed it from its tomb, while the relatives mourned as they had done on the day of burial. Only the bodies of those who had died recently were left as they were found. The rest were stripped of any remaining skin and flesh, which, along with the robes and mats in which they had been wrapped, were burned. This work was performed by the female relatives of the deceased, who are reported to have done it without manifesting any overt repugnance, although the corpses often were swarming with worms and smelled badly.

After the bones had been cleaned and washed, they were wrapped in fine new beaver pelts. The relatives of the deceased often collected skins specially for this purpose, even if it meant depriving themselves of skins needed for clothing or the fur trade. Relatives and friends contributed beads and necklaces to the bundle, saying, "I am giving this for the bones of my father [mother, or whatever relative it was]." The bundle was then put in a bag, decorated with necklaces, bracelets, and other ornaments, which a woman was able to carry on her back. Some of these bags were fashioned to resemble a person sitting in a crouching position. The whole bodies were wrapped in new skins and each was placed on a carrying frame. Then all the remains of the dead were taken back to the settlement, where each family gave a feast in honor of its own members. On this occasion, presents of skins, trade goods, and food were given to each dead person to honor his or her memory. These things were displayed in the house where the parcel containing the bones were kept. In some communities, a day or two before setting out for the Feast of the Dead, all the bones were brought to the house of an important chief, who offered a magnificent feast in honor of his predecessor or someone else of note. The presents that the relatives brought were displayed on poles along both sides of the longhouse, and all the guests shared their food with one another. At this feast the people imitated the cry of souls and left the house shouting "Haéé, haéé!"

After this, those who wished to attend the Feast of the Dead set out for the place where it was being held. The women, who on this occasion might travel considerable distances as part of their community's delegation, carried the bones of the dead in the parcels in which they had been wrapped. As the procession made its way along, the women repeated the cry of souls, saying that if they did not, the burden of the dead would weigh heavily on their backs and cause them to suffer from backaches for the rest of their lives. The procession moved slowly, stopping at each settlement along the way. As it approached a settlement, presents were exchanged, and each person went to the house of a relative, or clansperson, while the chiefs discussed how long the visitors would remain. In this way new friendships were made and old ones reaffirmed throughout the country.

In the town where the main ceremonies were to be held, the first seven or eight days were spent preparing all the bodies from the local cemetery, which would henceforth be abandoned, and welcoming the guests who were arriving from other villages. There were assigned hosts, in whose longhouses they placed the bones of their dead relatives and the gifts that accompanied them. There was continual feasting and dancing, and games were played, for which prizes were offered in the names of dead people. Women shot with a bow for prizes such as a porcupine quill collar or a string of wampum, and young men shot at sticks to win beaver pelts. Meanwhile, in a deserted cornfield not far from the settlement, a pit was dug about three meters deep and five meters or more in diameter (Kidd 1953). Around the pit, a carefully made scaffold or platform was erected that was up to fifteen meters across and three meters high, and ladders made of notched logs were put up all around it. Cross poles were erected on top of this platform to which the parcels containing the bones of the dead were later tied. The day preceding the start of the final interment ceremony, the undecomposed bodies were brought to the edge of the pit. They were placed underneath the scaffold on mats or slabs of bark fastened to stakes 1.5 meters or more high.

On the last day before the reburial of the dead, the packages containing their bones were taken down and opened so that their relatives might mourn over them again and wish them a final farewell. When the bundles were rewrapped, a few additional presents were sometimes added to them. One woman, for example, who was the daughter of an influential chief, placed his council sticks inside his bundle.

In the afternoon all of the people went to the field where the ossuary had been dug and arranged themselves according to settlements and clan segments (Fig.24). Each group then laid its parcels on the ground and, unfolding the presents that had been brought to honor the dead, hung them on poles where they remained on view for about two hours. At a Feast of the Dead held at Ossossané in 1636, over 1200 presents were displayed, most of them beaver robes. This display permitted non-Huron who were attending the feast to see the wealth of the country and gave each clan segment an opportunity to display its affluence and piety toward its dead. Less prosperous (often smaller) families deprived themselves of goods that they needed in order not to appear less generous or well-off than their neighbors.

Figure 24. A rather fanciful drawing of the Feast of the Dead prepared for Lafitau's Moeurs des sauvages, *1724.*

In the middle of the afternoon each of the chiefs, on receiving word from the chief who was in charge of the feast, gave a signal and all of his group, loaded with their parcels of bones, ascended the platform and hung them on the cross poles. Again, each settlement placed its bones in its own section. After that, the ladders were taken away, but a few chiefs remained on the platform. It was their duty to announce the presents that were being given to specified people on behalf of the dead. In this manner, many of the presents that had been put on display were redistributed to relatives and friends of the deceased and to those who had performed services for them, either by acting as hosts at the Feast of the Dead or by being the people who were in charge of a family's funerals. The formal announcements of these presents made it clear to everyone that each family had discharged its duty in this respect.

Toward evening about fifty beaver robes, each consisting of ten skins, were taken from among the presents that had been displayed, and used to line the burial pit. It is possible that one was donated by each of the clan segments that made up the Huron confederacy. These robes were arranged so that they extended a short distance beyond the edge of the pit all around. Some kettles as well as other objects, sometimes old and broken and other times in good condition, were put in the bottom of the pit for the use of the souls. Then the half-decayed, but entire bodies of the dead were lowered into the pit and arranged on the bottom. Besides the robe in which each of these corpses was wrapped, it was supplied with one, or even two, more robes to cover it.

All of the participants spent the night around the pit, lighting their fires and cooking their food on the spot. Normally, the bones of the dead were emptied into the pit at sunrise. However, if a package of bones accidentally fell into the pit, this was interpreted as a sign that the souls wished to be interred beforehand. At a given signal, people again mounted the platform and each person emptied his or her own package into the pit, keeping, however, the robes in which the bones had been wrapped. The grave goods that had been placed in the package with the bones were also thrown into the pit. At the same time, the crowd raised a great cry of lamentation. It was the duty of five or six men, stationed in the pit, to arrange the bones. This was done with poles in such a way as to mingle the bones of different individuals together to form a homogeneous mass.

When all the bones were thrown in, the pit was usually filled to within about sixty centimeters of the top. Then the robes bordering the edge were folded over them and the space in the center was covered with mats and pieces of bark. The mourners piled the sand that had been dug from the pit and some of the wooden poles that had been used to construct the platform on top of the grave to form a low mound. This was done to prevent animals from burrowing into it. Women brought dishes of corn which they threw on top of this mound to provide food for the souls of the dead. On that and following days, chiefs from the community where the Feast of the Dead had been celebrated made similar offerings.

The rest of the morning was spent distributing presents. Most of the robes in which the dead had been wrapped were sliced apart and the beaver skins that composed them were thrown from the platform into the midst of the crowd, who competed to get hold of them. When more than one person claimed the same skin, it was cut into several pieces. Twenty robes were given to the chief in charge of the feast, who used them to thank the chiefs of other groups who were present. Others were distributed by the chiefs of the clan segments to people whom the relatives of those being buried had designated. Still others, that had been used only for show, were taken away by the same people who had brought them.

Once these ceremonies were over, wooden stakes were driven into the ground around the perimeter of the ossuary, and the space they enclosed was roofed over. This hut, which either covered the mound or stood on top of it, was not rebuilt after the original one collapsed. It appears to have been a larger version of the ones that were erected in community cemeteries over the graves of people who were not intended to be reburied. These structures apparently were associated with a final interment.

When this work was finished, the participants feasted once again, and those who had come from elsewhere took their leave to return home. Everyone rejoiced that relatives and friends had received a fitting burial and been honored with so many presents. Much of the joy came from the renewal of old friendships and the reaffirmation of the ties that bound all the Huron peoples together. The solidarity of the participants was the greater because in one way or another everyone had been involved in giving and receiving presents. This, the Huron believed, was conducive to everyone's personal health and well-being, as well as the well-being of Huron society.

It would be a mistake, however, to stress the economic aspects of this ritual at the expense of other features. The great affection and concern that the Huron felt for the remains of those who had died in recent years and whose memory each Huron family cherished, was not a negligible factor. By joining in a common tribute to those who had died, the Huron were exercising a powerful force for promoting goodwill among the disparate segments of each community and of the confederacy as a whole. This was a force that came to be appreciated by some of the northern Algonkians with whom the Huron traded and had military alliances. As the Huron trading network expanded, the Feast of the Dead was extended to promote solidarity between the Huron and their allies, although the latters' subsistence patterns and cultures differed radically from their own. It is little wonder that during the seventeenth century this feast was adopted, albeit in a modified form, by the Nipissing and other northern peoples as a means of promoting political and commercial relations among themselves in the early days of the fur trade (Hickerson 1960). The last Feast of the Dead in which the Huron are reported to have participated seems to have been a joint Wyandot-Ottawa one held at Mackinac in 1695 (Kinietz 1940:117).

10/The Individual and Society

The Huron were greatly interested in averting illness and healing the sick. Many rituals and community activities were concerned with invoking supernatural aid for these purposes. A comparison with other northern Iroquoian cultures suggests that this concern was not simply the result of the epidemics of European diseases that ravaged this part of North America in the 1630s; rather it was a long-standing and important focus of Huron interest (Chafe 1964). While Huron methods for combating physical illnesses were of limited efficacy, their general view of sickness and health was far more sophisticated.

The Huron did not limit the concept of health to physical well-being, nor did they view individuals independently of their social environment. They drew no clear line between physical and mental states and did not attempt to distinguish between what happened to a person as the result of his own actions and what we would regard as accidents. The concept of health included an individual's happiness and sense of personal fulfillment, as well as his good or bad fortune. The Huron also equated health with generosity, which was one of the central values on which their society was based. It was therefore a concept that embraced everything that affected a human being both as an individual and as a member of society.

The Huron recognized three major causes of illness and mental disequilibrium: natural causes, witchcraft, and the unfulfilled desires of a person's soul. The latter were called *ondinnonk*.

Natural illnesses were those that the Huron were able to treat successfully by natural means. They were familiar with various herbs, roots, barks, and other plant medicines. One herb they valued highly was *oskar(a)*, perhaps wild sarsaparilla (*Aralia nudicalis*). It was used to treat wounds, ulcers, and open sores. *Oohrat*, the root of Indian turnip (*Arisaema triphyllum*), was used to clear phlegm from the sinuses of elderly people as well as to improve the complexion. It first had to be cooked in hot ashes to remove its stinging properties.

The Huron also used emetics and made incisions to drain swellings. Poultices were sometimes prescribed, and sweating was considered to be good for some ailments. Injuries, such as wounds caused by arrows and animal bites, were also treated by natural means, although spells frequently accompanied the cures. If treatment did not succeed, it was concluded that, in spite of appearances, the source of the problem was either witchcraft or soul desires.

DESIRES OF THE SOUL

According to Huron belief the health and fortune of individuals could be threatened both by other members of the community and by themselves. The theory of witchcraft assumed that diseases, as well as other misfortunes, were caused by spells that someone had cast upon the sick person. The cure for such diseases lay in extracting the spells that had been injected into people's bodies.

In addition, the life soul of every Huron was believed to possess concealed but powerful desires. Sometimes these desires were revealed to an individual in the form of dreams or visions, which were the means by which the life soul communicated its desires to the intellect soul. Even very young children had such desires, which were sometimes revealed to their parents in dreams. If these desires remained unfulfilled, the life soul became angry and this would cause its possessor to suffer illness and misfortune. Once a desire had been fulfilled, a person was expected to recover rapidly.

Sometimes the desire was for a particular item, such as a canoe, a wampum necklace, a dog, or some special kind of food. Desires of this sort played an important role in the *onnonhwaroia*. Other dreams gave promise of victory or warnings of danger which could be realized or averted only if certain desires of the soul were gratified. Still other dreams expressed the desire for socially unsanctioned forms of sexual gratification. A married man might wish to have a young girl come to him so that he could have sexual intercourse with her, or he might want to watch other people engaging in sexual relations. Such wishes were of particular significance, inasmuch as adult Huron were reluctant to talk about their sexual fantasies publicly. Another sort of dream wish that ran counter to the norms of Huron society expressed the hostility of one person toward another. In these dreams people were directed to humiliate, harm, or even kill someone else to prevent something bad happening to themselves. A final class of dreams involved offers by life souls to confer heightened powers upon individuals if they would perform certain rites or offer their soul specific presents. Often these presents had to be obtained from other people in the community. Individuals who had such dreams gave feasts to compel their souls to fulfill their promises as quickly as possible. Similar promises were also made in dreams by guardian spirits.

Dreams involving soul wishes and visitations by guardian spirits were common among both sexes. Wallace (1958) has noted that the majority of men's dreams fell into three classes. The first were associated with puberty and the achieving of adult status, the second with war, and the third with fears of old age and death. Huron women appear to have dreamed more often than men did. Their dreams frequently were concerned with the deaths of relatives. These dreams served to reveal some of the inner doubts and conflicts of those who had them.

SHAMANS

Although the Huron believed that their unfulfilled desires might reveal themselves in dreams, they were not always certain that their dreams had revealed the truth to them. Sometimes dreams were forgotten, or people failed to understand their real significance. In still other cases, the soul itself, or some malevolent spirit, might be seeking to mislead the dreamer. In order to interpret dreams properly, the help of a specialist was required.

The Huron recognized four kinds of shamans: those who were able to control the wind and rain, those who could predict future events, those who could find lost objects, and those who could heal the sick. Of these, the last were the most important. Only men appear to have served as curers; women who claimed supernatural powers restricted themselves to various forms of divination.

The general term for shaman was *arendiwannen*, meaning "his supernatural power is great." Arendiwannen who specialized in diagnosing ailments were called *okata* or *saokata*. These medicine men diagnosed and recommended treatments for all kinds of diseases. Each of them had an *oki* or guardian spirit who revealed to him the cause of an illness. Often this was done through dreams and visions that came immediately after waking. On other occasions, the *okata* determined the hidden desires of a person by gazing into a bowl full of water until the desire appeared to him. Others looked into fire, while still others fell into a frenzy, fasted, or secluded themselves in the darkness of a sweathouse. Sometimes a medicine man would sweat with ten or twenty other men in order to determine the nature of his patient's ailment. These shamans were believed to be able, with the support of their guardian spirits, to penetrate into their patients' souls and perceive their true desires, even those of children and ones which had long been forgotten. The man who accompanied the *okata*, carrying his drugs and turtle-shell rattle and who specialized in extracting spells, was called an *ontetsens* (see Chapter 7). Both kinds of medicine men were highly esteemed and well rewarded for their services.

Medicine men obtained their powers through visions or dreams in which a guardian spirit revealed itself to them. The Huron claimed that in former times a man who wished to become an *arendiwannen* fasted in seclusion for an entire month. During this period he saw no one except an assistant who brought him meager provisions and who likewise fasted. Even in the historical period, prolonged fasting and the avoidance of sexual activity were necessary for a guardian spirit to reveal itself to a would-be shaman. Some medicine men claimed a supernatural origin. Tonnerawannont, one of the famous medicine men of the Attignawantan, was a small hunchback who maintained that he was a spirit that had decided to become a human being. He left the subterranean abode where he had been living and entered the womb of the first woman he encountered. The woman, knowing that the child she bore had not been conceived by human means, induced an abortion. Then she wrapped the still living fetus in a beaver skin and abandoned it in the hollow of a tree. When a man passed by, the fetus cried out and he carried it back to the village, where the mother was able to adopt it. Tonnerawannont claimed that when he was still young, he had caused several children to die because they had ridiculed his physical deformity. This self-identification of a hunchback with a spirit was easy for the Huron to accept, because they pictured a number of their important mythological beings, including Iouskeha when he was the patron spirit of warriors, as dwarfs.

SATISFYING SOUL DESIRES

The Huron attempted to satisfy soul desires both to avoid and to cure illness. Soul desires were, for the most part, a request by individuals for something they did not have; hence, they could be satisfied only by someone else. Since the health and spiritual well-being of fellow Huron were at stake, the Huron felt obliged to help each other, insofar as this was possible, to satisfy their desires. Some desires, however, were impossible to satisfy in the form in which they were asked, either because the things that were requested could not be obtained, or because the desire itself was destructive toward the asker or other people. Yet not only the desires that were expressed but also the ways they could be satisfied were subject to social control. The Huron believed that in some cases soul desires could be satisfied symbolically, without providing or doing precisely what was requested.

The Huron alleged that sometimes when a medicine man was convinced that his patient was beyond recovery, he would suggest that the patient's soul desired things that he knew were impossible to obtain. In these cases, the person's death was attributed to society's failure to satisfy his inner wishes. In many cases, however, it was thought possible to substitute fewer items or ones that were more easily obtained for those that had been requested. In one case a mother dreamed that if her son was to be cured, he had to receive one hundred cakes of tobacco and four beaver skins. In place of these, it was decided that what he really needed were only ten cakes of tobacco and four large fish. In this way, individuals were prevented from making selfish and exhorbitant demands upon the community or using the institution as a means of self-aggrandizement. Substitution was also used to protect individuals. A desire to commit an act of violence might be fulfilled symbolically. We have already noted the case of a warrior who dreamed that he would be captured and burned at the stake. To avoid this he had his fellow villagers go through the preliminaries of torturing him, but at the climax of this ritual a dog was killed in his place. In such ways, the community was able to keep the destructive tendencies of soul desires under control.

Very often, when people were sick, a number of different ceremonies were thought necessary to satisfy the wishes of their souls. While anyone had the right to expect the community to show concern for his or her welfare, ceremonies involving the participation of large numbers of people appear to have been performed only for members of families to whom the community was socially indebted and who could provide food and gifts for the participants. Rituals involving the entire community had to receive the support of the local council. This does not mean, however, that anyone's needs went unanswered. While rituals that had large numbers of participants may, for that reason, have been regarded as more efficacious than smaller ones, healing primarily depended on an individual's dream being fulfilled. Therefore, so long as those who could claim less support kept their demands at an appropriate level, their well-being would be as well looked after as that of a socially prominent individual.

The basic curing ceremonies were highly stereotyped. In order to heal an individual, a particular society might be asked to perform its rituals, or a ceremony such as the *onnonhwaroia* was requested. Yet, on account of dreams, many personal variations were introduced into these rituals. A socially prominent woman, who seems to have been suffering from some kind of nervous disorder, claimed that when she went out of her house Aataentsik (the moon) appeared to her in the form of a tall and beautiful woman, who suggested that if the woman was to be cured all the surrounding peoples would have to offer her the distinctive products of their regions. Aataentsik also described specific ceremonies that were to be held in the woman's honor and told her that she should dress in red, so she would resemble the moon, which was made of fire. When she returned home, the woman became dizzy and suffered from severe muscle spasms. As a result, it was decided that an *onnonhwaroia* should be performed for her. Since she was not living in the settlement where she had been born, the chiefs of her natal community were asked to have this ceremony performed for her. They agreed, and the woman was carried to that settlement in a basket, accompanied by twenty or thirty singing people. When she arrived, she was approached by two men and two girls wearing special costumes and asked what she wanted. She named twenty-two presents, which the inhabitants of the settlement hastened to provide for her.

The chiefs then announced that everyone should keep their fires burning that evening and said that the patient had requested that they should be as large and bright as possible. After sunset, her muscles relaxed so she could walk. Supported by two people, she made her way down the center aisle of every longhouse in the community, in the course of which she passed through (or appeared to pass through) the middle of several hundred fires. In spite of this, she claimed that she felt little if any warmth. After this, the *onnonhwaroia* began. People painted themselves and ran through the village tossing furniture about, breaking pots, and knocking down dogs. For the next three days, these people had their dreams guessed. On the third day, the woman went through the houses again accompanied silently by a crowd of people. During this part of the ceremony, whoever was not accompanying her and having their dreams guessed was supposed to stay indoors. In each house she gave hints in the form of riddles concerning a last desire, which, when it was finally guessed, was an occasion for great rejoicing. She returned to all the houses a third time to thank everyone for her recovery, which it was believed must inevitably follow. At this time presents would have been distributed to the local people to thank them for what they had done. Then a community council was held at which the chiefs reviewed what had happened and gave the woman a final present to mark the end of the ceremony. In this instance we can see the regular observances of the *onnonhwaroia* being elaborated to satisfy the particular wishes of the individual for whom it was being celebrated. Such inventiveness not only increased the variety and interest of these feasts but also played an important part in the elaboration of Huron religion. Religious behavior was not regarded as static and highly formalized, but as vibrant and innovative. Personal variations as well as ideas borrowed from other cultures played an important role in modifying current practice.

A dog feast was sometimes requested by a patient or recommended by a shaman as a cure for illness. Since the dog that was killed and eaten in this ritual frequently, if not always, was regarded as a substitute for a human victim, there was a high degree of symbolism in this observance, in which the dog's life was offered as a substitute for that of the sick person. In the case of a young man afflicted by madness, two dogs were killed, one of which was especially dear to him.

Some of these requests could embarrass or inconvenience the participants. If an "eat all" feast was requested, the guests had to eat all the food, even though they might have to vomit up what they had eaten in order to finish the meal. Guests attending such feasts were not permitted to leave until they had consumed everything that was provided. At another kind of curing ceremony, the guests were asked to eat *andatarondi*, or bran biscuits, which produced a great deal of flatulence. It was believed that anyone who broke wind during this ceremony would soon die.

Other requests were overtly sexual in nature. When the young people of a community were asked to dance for the recovery of someone, they were often told how they should dress and paint themselves. It was also decided by the sick person or the shaman whether they should wear breach cloths or dance completely naked. In one instance a woman dreamed that she would be cured if all the young men and women danced naked in her presence and one of the men urinated in her mouth. In the hope of curing her, this ceremony was performed as she requested. The most sensational curing ritual of this sort was the *endakwandet*, which involved public sexual intercourse. This was a ceremony that seems to have been desired mainly by old men and women, and which may have expressed some of the envy that old people secretly felt for young ones in Huron society, despite the fact that old people were regarded as wiser and more reliable than the young. On one occasion all the young, unmarried girls in a village assembled in a sick woman's house and each was asked in turn to state with what young man she wished to have sexual intercourse. The men who were selected were notified by the chiefs who were in charge of the ceremony and came the next night to the woman's longhouse in order to have intercourse with these girls. They occupied the house from one end to the other and remained together until dawn. Throughout the night the sick woman, who was propped up at one end of the longhouse, watched the ceremony, while two chiefs or shamans, stationed at either end, shook their turtle-shell rattles and sang. In the case of an *endakwandet* that was performed for an old man, one girl was asked to have sexual intercourse with the patient. The *endakwandet* appears to have been a not uncommon ceremony and was viewed with public approval, even though the Huron normally disapproved of the public display of any sort of sexual behavior. This demonstrates how the Huron used curing rituals to transgress the restrictive norms of their society, albeit in well-defined and short-lived social contexts.

Not all dreams, however, made self-indulgent demands. Sometimes, at the *onnonhwaroia*, prosperous individuals dreamed that they were ordered to furnish their longhouses anew. To do this they and their families had to contrive to give away all of their household possessions to people who came to visit them. The search for health through giving conforms with the high value the Huron placed on generosity and parallels their custom of giving away property in an effort to avoid becoming the victims of witchcraft.

THE ROLE OF DREAMS

Not only in curing sickness but also in the normal course of their lives dreams (*yaracha*) played an important role. The Huron paid attention to their dreams when they went hunting, fishing, trading, and to war, as well as in their games, dances, and celebrations. The Jesuits described dreams as being the "real masters of the country." The answers to many problems of daily life were deliberately sought in dreams. Because dreams predicted future events and could warn people of dangers that threatened them, their advice might be followed in preference to that of leading chiefs. This was another means of protecting the independence of the individual and limiting the power of chiefs. Not all dreams were considered to be important, however, and not every dream was accepted as being true. In general, the public credence given to a dream varied according to the person's standing in his community. Likewise, if someone's dreams were to be widely believed, that person had to demonstrate that he or she could dream true on successive occasions.

Wallace (1958) has argued that the Huron concept of soul desires approximated a modern understanding of human psychology. He claims that the Huron distinguished the conscious and unconscious parts of the mind, recognized the power of unconscious longings, and were aware that the frustration of such desires could cause mental and physical illness. Their insistence that individuals were not always able to interpret the true meaning of their dreams also shows that they realized that desires often express themselves in symbolic forms. Thus they distinguished between the manifest and latent function of dreams.

In reality, the Huron conceptualized these relationships very differently from the way that modern psychologists do. Their belief that dreams and visions were the means by which souls communicated specific information to individuals about what was necessary for their physical and spiritual well-being has little in common with the modern notion that psychic disturbance arises from the frustration of basic drives. The belief that receiving material presents could resolve emotional tensions, which played such an important role in Huron curing, was also radically different from the analytical resolution of problems sought by modern psychotherapists. Moreover, the similarities between soul wishes and the advice of guardian spirits indicate that the Huron conceptualized what was happening in terms of a cosmology that was totally different from that of modern psychoanalysts.

The Huron furthermore regarded the satisfaction of soul desires as a process in which the community as well as the patient and the medical practitioner was involved. In a society where there were strong pressures on the individual to conform to social norms, the attribution of many personal frustrations and desires to forces that were not subject to their control provided people with a socially and psychologically acceptable outlet for their personal feelings. Through their soul desires, individuals who felt neglected, abused, or insecure could make claims upon the community for attention and psychological support. The ultimate aim of satisfying soul wishes was not, however, to alter the behavior of individuals but to modify their relations with society. This goal, which placed much of the responsibility for individual therapy upon the community, was in keeping with Huron belief in the integrity and rights of the individual.

In Huron society men in particular were expected to be self-reliant, brave, and uncomplaining. In everyday life they could ask for nothing for fear that this would compromise their independence and cast doubts on their manliness. Through their dreams, however, they could request support and attention without shame. Women faced rather different problems. Men were able to distinguish themselves as individuals in war, trade, and politics. A woman might win praise for being an industrious and efficient housewife, but the cooperative nature of life within matrilineal extended families did not provide the same scope for self-expression. Hence, women may have used their dreams as a means of claiming attention as individuals. It is indicative, however, of the relatively secure and respected position of women in Huron society that their dreams concerned the welfare of relatives more than they did their personal problems.

In the case of both men and women, soul desires appear to have helped to balance what might otherwise have become a very unequal relation between the individual and society. The demands that Huron society placed upon the individual for achievement and conformity could be countered by the demands that the individual made for attention and support upon the society as a whole through the medium of soul desires. From time to time these demands also permitted large numbers of people, whatever their status, to relax the narrow and normally strictly enforced conventions of their society and to gratify themselves in ways that were impermissible in terms of everyday life.

The indirect way in which society repaid its debt to the individual is further proof of Huron respect for individual dignity. Just as people could not be overtly coerced by any one person or group, although in reality they might be intimidated by public opinion, so they could not be openly supported. To have done so would have been to compromise the Hurons' cherished ideals of personal freedom and independence.

11/Epilogue

The Huron are notable for the high degree of economic equality they maintained, although they lived in communities that had as many as 2000 inhabitants and formed a settlement cluster of approximately 20,000 people. The Huron also believed that no person or group had the right to dominate or exploit another, or even to tell an individual what to do. In recent years, anthropologists have tended to restrict such equality to hunter-gatherer societies and to stress the hierarchical features of agricultural, and even sedentary collecting, groups (Testart 1982). Furthermore, they have emphasized the rapidity with which such egalitarian societies are transformed into hierarchical ones, as surviving hunter-gatherer peoples enter into close relations with more complex societies (Cashdan 1980). It is also claimed that the differences of age, gender, and individual prestige found in small-scale societies give rise to conflicts that resemble those that occur between classes in more complex ones (Bloch 1983). The questions to be answered are how and why did the Huron maintain a high degree of equality as their society grew larger and more complex?

Huron behavior, like that of all other human societies, was differentiated along lines of age, sex, and personal prestige. The division of labor was overwhelmingly along gender lines. Men cleared new fields, built houses, hunted, fished, waged war, and conducted the public affairs of their communities, peoples, and confederacy. Women planted, tended, and harvested crops; gathered firewood; cooked; looked after children; and engaged in craft production. Their role in hunting and fishing was limited to helping to process and transport some of the catch. In all of these activities, there was a strong emphasis on work teams made up of people of the same sex. Men frequently engaged in activities that took them far from their communities, while women rarely, if ever, ventured beyond the clearings that surrounded their communities unaccompanied by men.

There has been much debate about the respective power of men and women in Huron society and among the northern Iroquoian peoples generally (Brown 1970; Trigger 1978; Tooker 1984). These debates have traditionally revolved around the longstanding claim that Iroquoian society was matriarchal as well as matrilineal. While men held all public offices, they were elected to and could be dismissed from them by their matrilineal kinswomen. War chiefs and traders also had to obtain permission from women before they could take teenage boys away from their settlements. The strength of women was derived from living from birth to death in a single matrilocal extended family, while adult males had divided loyalties and obligations to the extended families into which they were born and into which they had married. Under these circumstances, women were more secure in their home life than men were.

Relations between mature men and women were characterized by considerable reserve and avoidance. When men felt unduly pressured by their female relatives to relocate a community so that it would be closer to fertile soil or sources of firewood, or to avenge a murdered kinsperson, they could disappear into the forest to hunt, fish, or trade. While Huron society was not the matriarchy that some people have imagined, men and women appear to have arranged their lives so that each had a significant input into most decisions about public policy and an appropriate measure of control over those matters that were of particular concern to them.

Relations between people of different ages were less equal than those between the sexes, although the impact was less serious since all Huron had the expectation of becoming more respected as they grew older. Older people served as heads and spokesmen for their extended families. Senior women played an important role in organizing female activities in such families and could bring pressure to bear on younger women to divorce a husband who was lazy or otherwise objectionable. Young men were not regarded as reliable witnesses or trustworthy bearers of messages, and political offices were held by mature men who had proved themselves worthy of them as hunters, orators, traders and, above all, warriors. On the other hand, children were never slapped, violently restrained, or seriously humiliated. The Huron believed that such treatment was immoral and might drive a young person to commit suicide. Social control of children was achieved indirectly, through praise, gentle ridicule, and inculcating feelings of guilt. Between people of all ages, care was taken to avoid the appearance that one person was being ordered about by another.

Chiefships were hereditary in certain lineages, although they were also achieved in the sense that there were no rules prescribing the individual order of inheritance of offices within a lineage. While chiefs and their families lived in more commodious longhouses and enjoyed more prestige than other people, they were expected to provide much of the food that was consumed during council meetings, public works projects such as erecting palisades, and an elaborate cycle of public celebrations and rituals. To produce this food a clan segment chief and the other members of his lineage had to work harder than other members of the clan segment, while members of clan segments that had a community or confederacy chief had to work harder than members of clan segments that did not. Although civil chiefs were in an advantageous position to obtain exotic goods (including imported tobacco) through diplomatic exchanges and foreign trade, they were required to distribute these goods generously to other Huron. Leaders had to win public approval by exhibiting self-restraint, wisdom, and generosity. A chief who lacked these qualities would have been unable to influence public opinion, however illustrious he and his family might have been.

The power of a chief was also limited by the Hurons' refusal to admit that any individual or group could be committed to a particular course of action unless they personally consented to it. The primary role of chiefs was as spokesmen for a collectivity; they did not have the power or the authority to impose their will on any member of their own or any other group. Discussion about matters of public policy continued until a consensus was reached that was agreed to by almost everyone. In the course of these debates, policies were modified until they received such approval. Even after this happened, there was no way in which chiefs could compel those individuals and groups that did not agree with a particular course of action to support it. Only public opinion, not leaders, might intimidate individuals or groups into supporting, or at least not opposing, a policy of which they did not approve.

The more popular chiefs were, and that generally meant the more generous, the easier it was for them to influence public debate. Yet any exhibition of arrogance or authoritarian behavior by a chief would have been met with widespread resistance. Even unintended slights and insults were a major threat to the Huron political order. Factionalism was rife and frequently caused communities to split apart along clan segment lines, while extended families sometimes moved from one community to another, normally joining a segment of the same clan in the other community. While most chiefs and their families worked hard to maintain their reputation for generosity, their aim was not, as it was among the chiefs of the Northwest Coast, to outdo and humiliate one another, since rivalry of this sort would have destroyed the delicate network of political alliances on which large communities and the entire Huron confederacy were based. The aim of their hard work and generosity was to reinforce their role as mediators and coordinators within and among clan segments, lineages, and extended families that refused to surrender any autonomy over their rights to manage their internal affairs. So powerful was this claim that not even a habitual murderer or thief could be personally punished except by his immediate family.

Ironically, the collecting peoples of the Northwest Coast, who normally lived in communities of only a few hundred people, exhibited a much higher level of concern for property, rank, and the exploitation of labor than did the Huron, or other Iroquoian groups, who had highly productive horticultural economies and lived in communities of up to 2000 people. On the Northwest Coast, prisoners of war became hereditary slaves, serving the needs of chiefly families. Among the Huron, such prisoners, when they were not killed, were adopted into families and might themselves become chiefs. The main explanation for this difference seems to be that, while the Indians of the Northwest Coast inhabited permanent base camps, exploited highly localized natural resources, and accumulated large quantities of possessions, the Huron were slash-and-burn horticulturalists. Their system of horticulture prevented them from staying in the same place for more than a few decades. Because of this, they lived in communities and houses that were not designed to last for generations and which could be constructed and replaced easily. Their possessions, likewise, were either portable or of a sort that could be easily replaced. The Huron population had probably reached the upper limits of what the region between Lake Ontario and Georgian Bay could have dependably supported in terms of fish and game; yet they cultivated only a tiny fraction of the arable land in that region. For defensive purposes and in order to share in a lucrative trade route with the north, the historical Huron preferred to live in a small part of Simcoe County that was protected from Iroquois attack by a perimeter of large settlements. Yet, from a horticultural point of view, they could more advantageously have been dispersed over a much wider area. During previous centuries, slash-and-burn horticulture and an abundance of arable land had created a situation in which it was impossible for any group to exploit or even offend the sensibilities of its neighbors, without the aggrieved group moving away. However strong the desire of the historical Huron may have been to form larger communities or to live closely together, it was not strong enough to overcome the readiness of Huron groups to relocate rather than to be humiliated by, or become subservient to, any group or individual.

It would, however, be a mistake to attribute the Huron preoccupation with personal independence and economic equality with a mechanical ecological causality. Pierre Clastres (1977) has argued against the belief that coercion and the subordination of one individual by another constitute the essence of power in all societies. He asserted that prior to the development of the state the locus of power was society as a whole. He further maintained that both struggles for supremacy between groups within such societies and the exercise of power by one individual over another were seen as tendencies that had to be resisted and subdued. In his opinion "primitive" people intuitively understand the danger of the state (even before it develops) and are prepared to use force to prevent the accumulation of private power. Despite the teleological difficulties with this formulation, it is clear that an elaborate set of positive and negative social sanctions which served to inhibit the development of economic and political inequality were deeply rooted in Huron culture.

Hard work and generosity were rewarded with tangible public approval. The Huron economy was structured in a fashion that made generosity highly visible. Exchanges of goods were essential features of public feasts, life-cycle ceremonies, curing rituals, community and personal religious celebrations, ritual friendships, settlements of disputes, and the conduct of diplomacy. These exchanges were so effective that there is no evidence that a barter system was needed to distribute goods. Moreover, if a longhouse burned down, the rest of the community competed in trying to compensate its inhabitants for their losses. Likewise, refugees were welcomed into Huron society and supported with food, clothing, and arable land until they could look after themselves. While ritual exchanges tended to even out disparities in the amount of goods possessed by individuals, the public nature of much of the giving, which included announcing the names of the donor and the recipient and the nature of the gift, ensured that those who were generous received full public recognition for what they had done. Mutual exchanges were also essential features of relations between neighboring groups that were not at war with each other.

On a religious plane, the Huron also associated generosity with health and peace and hence, with the well-being of their society. They believed that gifts would satisfy the hidden desires of people's souls and cure them of serious illnesses. Generosity among human beings was an extension of the generosity with which the forces of nature treated human beings by providing them with the life forces that were necessary to sustain their existence. This was a generosity that was reciprocated by the blood of warriors, whose sacrifice helped to maintain the cosmic cycle. Hence, people who were brave, industrious, and generous were seen as strengthening the creative forces of the universe. The vast redistributions that accompanied the Feast of the Dead expressed the concern of the living to honor and promote the spiritual well-being of the dead at the point where their souls were removed from regular contact with the living.

The Huron did not rely solely upon rewards to maintain their society; generosity was also reinforced by powerful negative sanctions. Sloth, greed, and other forms of antisocial behavior were the objects of censorious gossip which was much dreaded by the Huron, most of whom desired social approval more than anything else. Recalcitrant individuals, whose behavior was viewed as endangering the welfare of the community and the health of their neighbors, risked being accused of witchcraft, which meant that they were in league with malevolent supernatural forces. Like warfare, witchcraft was a manifestation of hostility and a desire to harm people. It also contradicted all the norms of generosity and cooperation on which social life was based. Hence, in order to protect themselves, the Huron had to hunt down and kill these hidden foes with the same determination that they waged war against the Iroquois.

Dread of inciting the hatred of witches and fear of being accused of practicing witchcraft were potent forces encouraging the Huron to live up to their society's ideals of generosity. While generosity was associated with friendship and life, stinginess and greed were associated with chaos and disruption. In this way, the key values of Huron society were linked to their view of the cosmic order and made sacred and inflexible.

Huron society encouraged hard work but also generosity and economic equality. Public opinion was intolerant of personal idiosyncracies, yet the Huron rejected the idea that any one Huron person or group had the right to try to coerce or intimidate another. Exhibitions of authoritarian behavior were repudiated as illegitimate and disruptive of public order. With their social institutions, their religious beliefs, and above all by manipulating gossip and witchcraft, the Huron articulated a potent set of mechanisms for defending their ideals of political and economic equality. In the Huron context these mechanisms were as effective for defending equality as the state has proved to be for defending private property and social inequality in hierarchical societies. While gossip and witchcraft become less effective for protecting equality as the scale of society increases, the self-reliance and mobility of Huron slash-and-burn horticulturalists allowed them to maintain a high degree of equality well beyond the point where it appears to have given way in societies that depended more heavily upon geographically restricted resources. In that respect the Huron resemble other slash-and-burn horticulturalists who have an abundance of arable land, such as the egalitarian (*gumloa*) Kachin of Burma (Leach 1954; cf. Friedman 1975) and more particularly the Tupi-Guarani peoples of lowland South America, who were the object of most of Clastres' (1977) research. The equality of Huron and Iroquois society was not a myth but the product of a system that was built upon positive and negative sanctions that, in their own way, were no less intricate and coercive than are those found in larger-scale state societies.

References

PUBLISHED SOURCES

Boucher, Pierre
1664 *Histoire véritable et naturelle des moeurs et productions du pays de la Nouvelle-France, vulgairement dite le Canada.* Paris: F. Lambert.

Champlain, Samuel de
1922–36 *The Works of Samuel de Champlain,* edited by H. P. Biggar. 6 vols. Toronto: The Champlain Society.

Chaumonot, Pierre
1869 *Le Père Pierre Chaumonot de la Compagnie de Jésus: autobiographie et pièces inédites.* Poitiers: H. Oudin.

Gendron, François
1868 *Quelques particularitez du pays des Hurons en la Nouvelle France remarquées par le Sieur Gendron, docteur en médecine qui a demeuré dans ce pays-là fort longtemps.* Albany, N.Y.: J. G. Shea.

Lafitau, Joseph François
1974–77 *Customs of the American Indians Compared with the Customs of Primitive Times,* edited and translated by W. N. Fenton and E. L. Moore. 2 vols. Toronto: The Champlain Society.

Le Clercq, Chrétien
1881 *First Establishment of the Faith in New France.* 2 vols. New York: J. G. Shea.

Poitier, Pierre
1920 "Elementa grammaticae huronicae, 1745"; "Radices huronicae," Facsimiles of Manuscripts in St. Mary's College, Montreal. Toronto: Fifteenth Report of the Bureau of Archives for the Province of Ontario.

Sagard, Gabriel
1866 *Histoire du Canada . . . avec un dictionnaire de la langue huronne.* 4 vols. Paris: Edwin Tross.
1939 *The Long Journey to the Country of the Hurons,* edited by G. M. Wrong. Toronto: The Champlain Society.

Thwaites, Reuben G., ed.
1896–1901 *The Jesuit Relations and Allied Documents.* 73 vols. Cleveland: Burrows Brothers.

STUDIES

Barbeau, Marius
   1960   *Huron-Wyandot Traditional Narratives in Translations and Native Texts*. Ottawa: National Museum of Canada, Bulletin No. 165.

Blau, Harold
   1966   "Function and the False Faces: A Classification of Onondaga Masked Rituals and Themes." *Journal of American Folklore* 79:564–580.

Bloch, Maurice
   1983   *Marxism and Anthropology*. Oxford: Oxford University Press.

Brown, J. K.
   1970   "Economic Organization and the Position of Women among the Iroquois." *Ethnohistory* 17:151–167.

Cashdan, E. A.
   1980   "Egalitarianism among Hunters and Gatherers." *American Anthropologist* 82:116–120.

Chafe, Wallace L.
   1964   "Linguistic Evidence for the Relative Age of Iroquois Religious Practices." *Southwestern Journal of Anthropology* 20:278–285.

Chapman, L. J. and D. F. Putnam
   1966   *The Physiography of Southern Ontario* (second edition). Toronto: University of Toronto Press.

Clastres, Pierre
   1977   *Society Against the State*. New York: Urizen Books.

Dobyns, Henry F.
   1983   *Their Number Become Thinned: Native American Population Dynamics in Eastern North America*. Knoxville: University of Tennessee Press.

Dodd, Christine F.
   1984   "Ontario Iroquois Tradition Longhouses." Ottawa: *Archaeological Survey of Canada, Mercury Series*, No. 124:181–437.

Ember, Melvin
   1973   "An Archaeological Indicator of Matrilocal versus Patrilocal Residence." *American Antiquity* 38:177–182.

Fenton, William N.
   1940   "Problems Arising from the Historic Northeastern Position of the Iroquois." Washington: *Smithsonian Miscellaneous Collections* 100:159–251.

Fox, William A.
   1980   "Miskwo Sinnee Munnidominug." *Archaeology of Eastern North America* 8:88–98.

Friedman, Jonathan
   1975   "Tribes, States, and Transformations." Maurice Bloch, ed. *Marxist Analyses and Social Anthropology:* 161–202. London: Malaby Press.

Gramly, R. M.
   1977   "Deerskins and Hunting Territories: Competition for a Scarce Resource of
   the Northeastern Woodlands." *American Antiquity* 42:601–605.

Hanzeli, V. E.
   1969   *Missionary Linguistics in New France*. The Hague: Mouton.

Heidenreich, Conrad E.
   1966   "Maps Relating to the First Half of the 17th Century and their Use in
   Determining the Location of Jesuit Missions in Huronia." *The Cartographer*
   3:103–126.
   1967   "The Indian Occupance of Huronia 1600–1650." R.Louis Gentilcore, ed.
   Canada's Changing Geography: 15–29. Scarborough, Ontario: Prentice-Hall
   of Canada.
   1971   *Huronia: A History and Geography of the Huron Indians, 1600–1650*. Toronto: McClelland and Stewart.
   1974   "A Relict Indian Corn Field near Creemore, Ontario." *Canadian Geographer*
   18(4):379–394.

Hickerson, Harold
   1960   "The Feast of the Dead among the Seventeenth Century Algonkians of the
   Upper Great Lakes." *American Anthropologist* 62:81–107.

Hoffman, D. W., R. E. Wicklund, and N. R. Richards
   1962   *Soil Survey of Simcoe County, Ontario*. Ottawa and Guelph: Ontario Soil
   Survey, Report no. 29.

Jackes, Mary
   1986   "The Mortality of Ontario Archaeological Populations." *Canadian Journal
   of Anthropology* 5(2):33–48.

Kidd, Kenneth E.
   1949   *The Excavation of Ste. Marie I*. Toronto: University of Toronto Press.
   1953   "The Excavation and Historical Identification of a Huron Ossuary." *American Antiquity* 18:359–379.

Kinietz, W. Vernon
   1940   *The Indians of the Western Great Lakes, 1615–1760*. Ann Arbor: University
   of Michigan Press.

Knowles, Nathaniel
   1940   "The Torture of Captives by the Indians of Eastern North America." Philadelphia: *Proceedings of the American Philosophical Society* 82:151–225.

Latta, Martha A.
   1985   "Identification of the 17th Century French Missions in Eastern Huronia."
   Canadian Journal of Archaeology 9:147–171.

Leach, Edmund R.
   1954   *Political Systems of Highland Burma*. Cambridge: Harvard University Press.

Lounsbury, Floyd G.
   1978   "Iroquoian Languages." Bruce G. Trigger, ed. *Handbook of North American
   Indians*, Vol. 15, *Northeast*, pp. 334–343. Washington: Smithsonian Institution.

MacNeish, Richard S.
  1952 *Iroquois Pottery Types*. Ottawa: National Museum of Canada, Bulletin No. 124.

McPherron, Alan
  1967 "On the Sociology of Ceramics: Pottery Style Clustering, Marital Residence, and Cultural Adaptations of an Algonkian-Iroquoian Border." Elisabeth Tooker, ed. *Iroquois Culture, History, and Prehistory*, pp. 101–107. Albany: The University of the State of New York.

Molto, J. E.
  1983 *Biological Relationships of Southern Ontario Woodland Peoples: The Evidence of Discontinuous Cranial Morphology*. Ottawa: *Archaeological Survey of Canada, Mercury Series*, No. 117.

Morgan, Lewis H.
  1871 *Systems of Consanguinity and Affinity of the Human Family*. Washington: Smithsonian Contributions to Knowledge, Vol. 17.

Norcliffe, G. B. and C. E. Heidenreich
  1974 "The Preferred Orientation of Iroquoian Longhouses in Ontario." *Ontario Archaeology* 23:3–30.

Parkman, Francis
  1867 *The Jesuits in North America in the Seventeenth Century*. Boston: Little, Brown and Co.

Patterson, D. K., Jr.
  1984 *A Diachronic Study of Dental Palaeopathology and Attritional Status of Prehistoric Ontario Pre-Iroquois and Iroquois Populations*. Ottawa: *Archaeological Survey of Canada, Mercury Series*, No. 122.

Pendergast, James F.
  1989 "The Significance of Some Marine Shell Excavated on Iroquoian Archaeological Sites in Ontario." C. F. Hayes III, ed. *Proceedings of the 1986 Shell Bead Conference*, pp. 97–112. Rochester: Rochester Museum and Science Center, Research Records, 20.

Pendergast, James F. and B. G. Trigger
  1972 *Cartier's Hochelaga and the Dawson Site*. Montreal: McGill-Queen's University Press.

Pfeiffer, Susan
  1986 "Morbidity and Mortality in the Uxbridge Ossuary." *Canadian Journal of Anthropology* 5(2):23–31.

Pfeiffer, Susan and P. King
  1983 "Cortical Bone Formation and Diet among Protohistoric Iroquoians." *American Journal of Physical Anthropology* 60:23–28.

Ramsden, Peter G.
  1977 *A Refinement of Some Aspects of Huron Ceramic Analysis*. Ottawa: *Archaeological Survey of Canada, Mercury Series*, No. 63.

Rands, Robert L. and Carroll L. Riley
 1958 "Diffusion and Discontinuous Distribution." *American Anthropologist*
   60:274–297.

Richards, Cara
 1967 "Huron and Iroquois Residence Patterns, 1600–1650." Elisabeth Tooker,
   ed. *Iroquois Culture, History, and Prehistory*, pp. 51–56. Albany: The University of the State of New York.

Ridley, Frank
 1954 "The Frank Bay Site, Lake Nipissing, Ontario." *American Antiquity*
   20:40–50.
 1961 *Archaeology of the Neutral Indians*. Port Credit, Ontario: Etobicoke Historical Society.

Snow, Dean R. and W. A. Starna
 1989 "Sixteenth-Century Depopulation: A View from the Mohawk Valley."
   American Anthropologist 91:142–149.

Spence, Michael W.
 1986 "Band Structure and Interaction in Early Southern Ontario." *Canadian Journal of Anthropology* 5(2):83–95.

Steckley, John
 1978 "The Soul Concepts of the Huron." M.A. thesis, Memorial University of
   Newfoundland, St. John's, Newfoundland.
 1982a "The Clans and Phratries of the Huron." *Ontario Archaeology* 37:29–34.
 1982b "The Cord Tribe of the Huron." *Arch Notes, Newsletter of the Ontario
   Archaeological Society* 82(6):15.
 1983 "The Huron Calendar." *Arch Notes* 83(1):11–13.
 1986a "Were Burbot Important to the Huron?" *Arch Notes* 86(1):19–23.
 1986b "Whose Child is This? Speculation Concerning Huron Infant Burial." *Arch
   Notes* 86(5):5-8.
 1987a "An Ethnolinguistic Look at the Huron Longhouse." *Ontario Archaeology*
   47:19–32.
 1987b "Huron Armour." *Arch Notes* 87(5):7–11.
 1989 "Huron Sweat Lodges: The Linguistic Evidence." *Arch Notes* 89(1):7–8.

Testart, Alain
 1982 *Les chasseurs-cueilleurs, ou, l'origine des inégalités*. Paris: Société d'Ethno-
   graphie, Memoires, 26.

Tooker, Elisabeth
 1960 "Three Aspects of Northern Iroquoian Culture Change." *Pennsylvania Archaeologist* 30(2):65–71.
 1964 *An Ethnography of the Huron Indians, 1615–1649*. Washington: Bureau of
   American Ethnology, Bulletin No. 190.
 1968 "Sibs, Clans, Gentes, Tribes, Nations and Related Matters." *Bulletin of the
   Philadelphia Anthropological Society* 19(2):14–17.
 1970 "Northern Iroquoian Sociopolitical Organization." *American Anthropologist*
   72:90–97.
 1984 "Women in Iroquois Society." M. K. Foster *et al.*, eds. *Extending the Rafters:*

Interdisciplinary Approaches to Iroquoian Studies, pp. 109–123. Albany: State University of New York Press.

Trigger, Bruce G.
  1962 "The Historic Location of the Hurons." *Ontario History* 54:137–148.
  1976 *The Children of Aataentsic: A History of the Huron People to 1660.* Montreal: McGill-Queen's University Press.
  1978 "Iroquoian Matriliny." *Pennsylvania Archaeologist* 48(1–2):55–65.
  1985 *Natives and Newcomers: Canada's "Heroic Age" Reconsidered.* Montreal: McGill-Queen's University Press.

Vincent Tehariolina, Marguerite
  1984 *La Nation Huronne.* Quebec: Editions du Pélican.

Wallace, Anthony F. C.
  1958 "Dreams and the Wishes of the Soul: A Type of Psychoanalytic Theory among the Seventeenth Century Iroquois." *American Anthropologist* 60:234–248.
  1970 *The Death and Rebirth of the Seneca.* New York: Knopf.

Warrick, Gary A.
  1984 "Reconstructing Ontario Iroquoian Village Organization." Ottawa: *Archaeological Survey of Canada, Mercury Series*, No. 124:1–180.
  1988 "Estimating Ontario Iroquoian Village Duration." *Man in the Northeast* 36:21–60.
  1989 "A Population History of the Huron-Petun, A.D. 900–1650." Ph.D. dissertation, McGill University, Montreal.

Witthoft, John
  1959 "Ancestry of the Susquehannocks." John Witthoft and W. F. Kinsey III, eds. *Susquehannock Miscellany*, pp. 19–60. Harrisburg: The Pennsylvania Historical and Museum Commission.

Wright, James V.
  1966 *The Ontario Iroquois Tradition.* Ottawa: National Museum of Canada, Bulletin no. 210.

Recommended Reading

Barbeau, Charles Marius, 1915. *Huron and Wyandot Mythology*. Ottawa: Department of Mines, Geological Survey, Memoir No. 80.
A collection of Wyandot tales recorded from native speakers in Oklahoma and Ontario early in the twentieth century.

Heidenreich, Conrad E., 1971. *Huronia: A History and Geography of the Huron Indians, 1600–1650*. Toronto: McClelland and Stewart.
A magisterial study of Huron geography and cultural ecology.

Jaenen, Cornelius, 1976. *Friend and Foe: Aspects of French-Amerindian Cultural Contact in the Sixteenth and Seventeenth Centuries*. Toronto: McClelland and Stewart.
A general survey of relations between native groups, including the Huron, and the French during the early periods of direct contact.

Tooker, Elisabeth, 1964. *An Ethnography of the Huron Indians, 1615–1649*. Washington: Bureau of American Ethnology, Bulletin No. 190.
This source book presents a carefully organized paraphrase of all the data about the Huron contained in the writings of Champlain, Sagard, and the Jesuit *Relations*, along with notes comparing these data with Iroquois and Wyandot culture. For a list of minor corrections, see E. Tooker, "Corrigenda to Tooker: An Ethnography of the Huron Indians, 1615–1649." *Man in the Northeast* 36 (1988):109–110.

Trigger, Bruce G., 1976. *The Children of Aataentsic: A History of the Huron People to 1660*. Montreal: McGill-Queen's University Press (reprinted 1987).
A history of the Huron from earliest times until the decade following their dispersal by the Iroquois in 1649.

———, Volume editor, 1978. *Handbook of North American Indians*, Volume 15, *Northeast*. Washington, D.C.: Smithsonian Institution.
A comprehensive set of papers surveying the archaeology, languages, history, culture, and modern conditions of the native inhabitants of the northeastern Woodlands of North America, including all of the northern Iroquoians. W. N. Fenton's "Northern Iroquoian Culture Patterns" (pp. 296–321) provides the best general survey of northern Iroquoian culture available anywhere.

———, 1985. *Natives and Newcomers: Canada's "Heroic Age" Reconsidered*. Montreal: McGill-Queen's University Press.
A study of methodological problems relating to the investigation of the historical ethnography and ethnohistory of native peoples, with special reference to the Huron.

Vincent Tehariolina, Marguerite, 1984. *La Nation Huronne: Son Histoire, Sa Culture, Son Esprit*. Quebec: Editions du Pélican.
Essays on Huron history and culture by a modern Huron living near Quebec City. This material is based partly on written records and partly on local traditions and contains many interesting personal observations.

Wright, James V., 1966. *The Ontario Iroquois Tradition*. Ottawa: National Museum of Canada, Bulletin No. 210.

A synthesis of archaeological data pertaining to the prehistoric development of Iroquoian culture in Ontario. Now somewhat out-of-date, but still the best available. For more recent material, see J. V. Wright, 1987. "Iroquoian Agricultural Settlement," R. Cole Harris, ed. *Historical Atlas of Canada*, Vol. 1, Plate 12.

Index